MAYA ANGELOU

OVERCOMING ADVERSITY

MAYA ANGELOU

Pamela Loos

Introduction by James Scott Brady,
Trustee, the Center to Prevent Handgun Violence
Vice Chairman, the Brain Injury Foundation

Chelsea House Publishers
Philadelphia

Frontis: Maya Angelou's success as a poet, autobiographical writer, film director, actress, singer, and producer are a testament to her self-confidence and determination.

CHELSEA HOUSE PUBLISHERS

EDITOR IN CHIEF Stephen Reginald
PRODUCTION MANAGER Pamela Loos
DIRECTOR OF PHOTOGRAPHY Judy L. Hasday
ART DIRECTOR Sara Davis
MANAGING EDITOR James D. Gallagher
SENIOR PRODUCTION EDITOR LeeAnne Gelletly

Staff for **Maya Angelou**
PROJECT EDITOR Therese De Angelis
CONTRIBUTING EDITOR James D. Gallagher
ASSOCIATE ART DIRECTOR Takeshi Takahashi
DESIGNER 21st Century Publishing and Communications, Inc.
PICTURE RESEARCHER Patricia Burns
COVER ILLUSTRATOR Earl Parker
COVER DESIGNER Brian Wible

The Chelsea House World Wide Website address is http://www.chelseahouse.com

First Printing

1 3 5 7 9 8 6 4 2

Library of Congress Cataloging-in-Publication Data

Loos, Pamela.
Maya Angelou / Pamela Loos.
    pp.   cm. — (Overcoming adversity)
Summary: Describes the life and writing career of the author of "I Know Why the Caged Bird Sings," as well as her victory over such obstacles as prejudice, poverty, and rape.
ISBN 0-7910-4946-9 (hc). — ISBN 0-7910-4947-7 (pb)
1. Angelou, Maya—Juvenile literature. 2. Women authors, American—20th century—Biography—Juvenile literature. 3. Women civil rights workers—United States—Biography—Juvenile literature. 4. Afro-American women authors—Biography—Juvenile literature. [1. Angelou, Maya. 2. Authors, American. 3. Afro-Americans—Biography. 4. Women—Biography.] I. Title. II. Series.
PS3551.N464Z756 1999
818'.5409—dc21
[B]   99–19890
                                                      CIP

CONTENTS

OVERCOMING ADVERSITY

ON FACING ADVERSITY

James Scott Brady

I GUESS IT'S a long way from a Centralia, Illinois, train yard to the George Washington University Hospital Trauma Unit. My dad was a yardmaster for the old Chicago, Burlington & Quincy Railroad. As a child, I used to get to sit in the engineer's lap and imagine what it was like to drive that train. I guess I always have liked being in the "driver's seat."

Years later, however, my interest turned from driving trains to driving campaigns. In 1979, former Texas governor John Connally hired me as a press secretary in his campaign for the American presidency. We lost the Republican primary to a former Hollywood star named Ronald Reagan. But I managed to jump over to the Reagan campaign. When Reagan was elected in 1980, I was "sitting in the catbird seat," as humorist James Thurber would say—poised to be named presidential press secretary. I held that title throughout the eight years of the Reagan administration. But not without one terrible, extended interruption.

It happened barely two months after the Reagan administration took office. I never even heard the shots. On March 30, 1981, my life went blank in an instant. In an attempt to assassinate President Reagan, John Hinckley Jr. armed himself with a "Saturday night special"—a low-quality, $29 pistol—and shot wildly as our presidential entourage exited a Washington hotel. One of the exploding bullets struck me just above the left eye. It shattered into a couple dozen fragments, some of which penetrated my skull and entered my brain.

The next few months of my life were a nightmare of repeated surgery, broken contact with the outside world, and a variety of medical complications. More than once, I was very close to death.

The next few years were filled with frustrating struggles to function with a paralyzed right side, struggles to speak and communicate.

To people who face and defeat daunting obstacles, "ambition" is not becoming wealthy or famous or winning elections or awards. Words like "ambition" and "achievement" and "success" take on very different meanings. The objective is just to live, to wake up every morning. The goals are not lofty; they are very ordinary.

My own heroes are ordinary folks—but they accomplish extraordinary things because they try. My greatest hero is my wife, Sarah. She's accomplished a lot of things in life, but two stand out. The first has been the way she has cared for me and our son since I was shot. A tremendous tragedy and burden was dropped unexpectedly into her life, totally beyond her control and without justification. She could have given up; instead, she focused her energies on preserving our family and returning our lives to normal as much as possible. Week by week, month by month, year by year, she has not reached for the miraculous, just for the normal. Yet in focusing on the normal, she has helped accomplish the miraculous.

Her other most remarkable accomplishment, to me, has been spearheading the effort to keep guns out of the hands of criminals and children in America. Opponents call her a "gun grabber"; I call her a national hero. And I am not alone.

After a seven-year battle, during which Sarah and I worked tirelessly to educate the public about the need for stronger gun laws, the Brady Bill became law in 1993. It was a victory, achieved in the face of tremendous opposition, that now benefits all Americans. From the time the law took effect through fall 1997, background checks had stopped 173,000 criminals and other high-risk purchasers from buying handguns, and the law has helped to reduce illegal gun trafficking.

Sarah was not pursuing fame, or even recognition. She simply started at one point—when our son, Scott, found a loaded handgun on the seat of a pickup truck and, thinking it was a toy, pointed it at Sarah.

Fortunately, no one was hurt. But seeing a gun nearly bring a second tragedy upon our family, Sarah became determined to do whatever she could to prevent senseless death and injury from guns.

Some people think of Sarah as a powerful political force. To me, she's the person who so many times fed me and helped me dress during my long years of recovery.

Overcoming obstacles is part of life, not just for people who are challenged by disabilities, illnesses, or tragedies, but for all people. No matter what the obstacle—fear, disability, prejudice, grief, or a difficulty that isn't likely to "just go away"—we can all work to make this world a better place.

Maya Angelou in a pensive moment. The poet contemplated her difficult childhood in her best-known work, the autobiographical I Know Why the Caged Bird Sings, *published in 1970.*

1

TRAUMA

"There's not been a day . . . [that] I have not thought of it."

—Maya Angelou, 50 years after being raped

FOR AS LONG as she could remember, her mother had been dead. For a sensitive six-year-old, the knowledge was a terrible weight to carry. And the weight felt even heavier to Marguerite Johnson (who later renamed herself Maya Angelou) when she realized that it also rested on the slender shoulders of her young brother.

But one cool December in Stamps, Arkansas, where Marguerite lived with her brother, Bailey—her favorite person—and their paternal grandmother, Annie Henderson, Marguerite was confronted with the notion that her mother might be alive after all. Far from making her happy, however, the revelation made the painful weight she had been bearing only feel worse. How could it be, she thought, that Mother could be alive and not want to be with Bailey and me?

That Christmas in 1934, Mrs. Henderson, whom the children called Momma, explained that Mother and Father had sent them presents. She told them that their parents—her son, Bailey Johnson, and Vivian Baxter, were divorced and lived in different parts of the glorious state of California. There, Momma told them, "they could have all the oranges they could eat. And the sun shone all the time," Marguerite wrote in *I Know Why the Caged Bird Sings.* Momma explained, too, that Mother and Father had sent them back to Arkansas a few years earlier so that she could take care of them. "I was sure that wasn't so," Marguerite wrote. "I couldn't believe that our mother would laugh and eat oranges in the sunshine without her children. Until that Christmas . . . I could cry anytime I wanted by picturing my mother (I didn't quite know what she looked like) lying in her coffin. . . . The face was brown, like a big O, and since I couldn't fill in the features I printed MOTHER across the O, and tears would fall down my cheeks like warm milk."

Momma's explanation only created stinging questions for Marguerite. Why had her parents sent Bailey and her away? The only possible explanation was that they had done something very, very wrong. What could it have been? Why had they been sent alone by train, with identifying tags on their wrists, from California to Arkansas when they were only three and four years old?

Bailey helped Marguerite and himself ease the pain and confusion over their parents by tearing the stuffing out of a doll their parents had sent. But they kept the other gifts in good condition. After all, perhaps their parents had changed their minds and decided they wanted their children back. Any day now, they could pull up the dusty road leading to the house, filled with forgiveness and ready to give out years of missed hugs. When they did, they would want to know how their children were enjoying their presents.

Years later, in a conversation with her friend Rosa Guy that was published in *Writing Lives: Conversations Between Women Writers* (1988), Maya talked about how she managed the anger she felt toward her mother for seeing her only once when she was between the ages of three and 13:

> I haven't stopped being angry at a number of things. . . .
> But I think the reason I've been able to be successful, not
> just as a writer, but as a woman and as a person is that at
> about twenty-two . . . for some incredible reason, I saw
> my mother separate from me. Absolutely separate. And I
> thought, I see, you're not really my mother, the mother I
> wanted and needed; you're a character. And I began to see
> her like a character I would have read about. Now that
> didn't mean that in lonely or bitter or painful moments I
> didn't still want her to be that big-bosomed, open-armed,
> steady, consistent person. But I'd say that 60 percent of
> the time I saw her as a character. Then it grew to be 70
> per cent. Then 80. And then my own resistance allowed
> me to accept her as the character.

A year after that Christmas in 1934, Bailey and Marguerite's father appeared just as they had suspected he would—with no warning except the popping sound of crunched stones and the commotion he raised as his car made its way up their dirt road. Once he took Bailey in one arm and Marguerite in the other, all of their bitterness toward him seemed to quickly melt. Seven-year-old Marguerite was proud of his handsome face, nice car, and fancy clothes. He certainly must be rich; maybe he even lived in a castle, she thought. And he surely must love his children if he came all the way to Arkansas from California. Still, he was so good-looking that Marguerite began to worry that she was adopted.

For three weeks, Bailey Johnson Sr. received the attention of Stamps's residents. Then he announced that he had to return to California. By this time, Marguerite was

This lumber mill and a cotton-processing facility were the only two industries in Stamps, Arkansas, where Marguerite and her brother, Bailey, lived with their grandmother when they were children.

relieved. "My world was going to be emptier and dryer, but the agony of having him intrude into every private second would be gone," she recalled in *I Know Why the Caged Bird Sings.* "I wouldn't have to wonder whether I loved him or not." But then she learned that her father intended to take his children with him! While Bailey was eager to go, Marguerite was hesitant. Finally she gave in and found herself crammed into the back seat of her father's car, confronted with the clashing aromas of boxes, luggage, fried chicken, and sweet potato pie. Bailey, meanwhile, was in the front seat "buttering up" their father. It was only after they had been driving for a while that Father announced that they were actually going to see their mother in St. Louis, Missouri. Marguerite cried, and she wondered how Bailey could compose himself. But there was no turning back, even though she begged. They were on their way to Mother's house.

"To describe my mother would be to write about a hurricane in its perfect power," Maya Angelou wrote years later. "My mother's beauty literally assailed me. . . . Her smile widened her mouth beyond her cheeks beyond her ears and seemingly through the walls to the street outside. I was struck dumb. I knew immediately why she had sent me away. She was too beautiful to have children."

Bailey Sr. left St. Louis within a few days, leaving his children to start new lives in a strange new place. Marguerite and Bailey quickly became acquainted with Mother's family. Grandmother Baxter was a respected and feared police precinct captain, who had great clout with the police department, city government, and courts. Her brothers were all known to be quite mean, and Grandfather Baxter was a hard man, although he had recently become bedridden. And the city itself was a rough place, where underworld life was barely kept under—a far cry from the rural friendliness of Stamps.

For six months the children lived with their grandparents; then they moved in with Vivian Baxter and her boyfriend, whom the children knew only as Mr. Freeman. Mother gave the children their own rooms, plenty to eat, and store-bought clothes. Marguerite became so nervous about the changes that she became a shadow of herself, moving and speaking with extreme care at all times, fearful of saying or doing something that would make her mother ship her back to Arkansas.

Constance Good, as seven-year-old Marguerite "Maya" Johnson, confronts the man who raped her in the 1979 television movie I Know Why the Caged Bird Sings. *"Mr. Freeman had surely done something wrong, but I was convinced that I had helped him do it," Maya Angelou later wrote about her confused feelings.*

Although Mother was a nurse, she never worked as one while Marguerite and Bailey lived with her. Instead, she usually made a living by running illegal card games, an occupation for which she was unapologetic. After all, she told her children, it was a more honest living than most of the jobs that were open to black women at the time—and she never cheated anyone, she added. Mr. Freeman, who was a foreman in the Southern Pacific railroad yards, paid most of the family's expenses. Mr. Freeman left the children to themselves; Vivian had trained them to do their homework right after school and clean up the dinner dishes before they could read or listen to the radio.

The displaced children developed troublesome afflictions—Bailey began to stutter, and Marguerite had frequent nightmares. When Marguerite got scared at night, she would take solace in her mother's bed. One morning she woke up to find her mother gone and Mr. Freeman lying right next to her. Before she realized what was happening, he pulled her on top of his chest and aroused himself. She was terrified; his heart was beating very hard and she had heard ghost stories of people who died and could not let go of what they were last holding.

But when Mr. Freeman relaxed, the young girl, starved for affection, felt strangely at home. "He held me so softly that I wished he wouldn't ever let me go," she said in *I Know Why the Caged Bird Sings.* She even wondered whether she had found her real father at last.

Marguerite was even more confused when Mr. Freeman threatened to kill Bailey if she told anyone what had happened. After all, what had happened? She wasn't even sure. It was the first secret she had ever kept from Bailey.

For months afterward, Mr. Freeman would not speak to her. Then, one late spring afternoon when Bailey was out playing baseball and Mother was away, Mr. Freeman pulled Marguerite to him again in the big living room chair. He turned up the radio very loud, told her he would kill her if she made a sound, and threatened again to kill her brother if she told anyone about what was happening. And then he raped her. She was just seven-and-a-half years old.

Marguerite felt so much pain that she blacked out. When she came to, Mr. Freeman was washing her in the bathtub. Although he claimed that he hadn't meant to hurt her, he kept insisting that she couldn't tell anyone what had happened. Then he told her to go to the library as she normally did, and to act natural.

But she couldn't. Her hips felt like they were coming out of their sockets. Her legs throbbed. Her stomach felt like it was on fire. She came back home and went to bed and said nothing to allay her mother's concern that she had the measles. When her mother lifted Marguerite's sweaty body from the bed and saw blood stains, she took her daughter to the hospital. Only after Bailey assured his sister that no one would kill him, no matter what, did Marguerite tell who had hurt her. Mr. Freeman was arrested.

Marguerite had to go to court and answer questions about the rape. She didn't know how to answer some of them. She didn't want people to think she had done something wrong, but it was clear to her that Mr. Freeman *had*, and she convinced herself that she had helped him do it. So when the lawyer asked her whether Mr. Freeman had ever touched her before the day she was raped, Marguerite said no. Mr. Freeman was sentenced to one year in prison but somehow managed to get released that very afternoon. Later that day, he was found dead behind a local slaughterhouse. People claimed he had been kicked to death.

Marguerite decided that Mr. Freeman was dead because she had lied in court. She thought she had made the bad thing that had happened even worse. Apparently, she thought, her words could kill people. "Obviously I had forfeited my place in heaven forever," Maya Angelou wrote in *I Know Why the Caged Bird Sings*, "and I was as gutless as the doll I had ripped to pieces ages ago. Even Christ Himself turned His back on Satan. Wouldn't He turn His back on me? I could feel the evilness flowing through my body."

Marguerite decided she could talk to no one but Bailey. After the doctor pronounced her healed, her family seemed to want Marguerite to bounce back to her old self. But she couldn't. She didn't feel the same. They punished—and sometimes thrashed—her for not talking, and she retreated even further into silence.

After only eight months, Marguerite and Bailey were sent back to Arkansas. Bailey cried desperately on the train, and Marguerite felt even worse. She would remain nearly silent, except to speak to Bailey, for about five years.

In a 1987 interview with the *Los Angeles Herald Examiner*, Maya Angelou spoke about the horror of rape and how she learned to live with it by "trying to understand how really sick and alone that man [who raped her] was. I don't mean that I condone at all. But to try to understand is always healing."

"Still," she added, "there's not been a day since the rape 50 years ago during which I have not thought of it."

Today, Maya Angelou's poetic readings stir and inspire her listeners. However, as a child trauma-tized by rape, Maya Johnson's voice was stilled. She later admitted that she hid inside a "cocoon" of silence for nearly five years.

2

A LIFE LINE

"I was liked . . . for just being Marguerite Johnson."

—I Know Why the Caged Bird Sings, 1970

"INTO THIS COCOON I crept," Maya Angelou wrote about withdrawing into muteness in *I Know Why the Caged Bird Sings*. She felt safer when she was silent, and also just by being back in Stamps. There were no tall buildings, noisy cabs and trucks, or bustling family gatherings. In Stamps, she thought, nothing ever happened, so nothing else could hurt her. And unlike her mother's relatives, people in Stamps accepted her muteness. After all, they supposed, she was only trying to adjust to being back in the South, and she had been so delicate to begin with, others agreed. No one in Stamps knew what had happened to Marguerite in St. Louis except Momma. To help her granddaughter communicate, Momma

In this scene from the 1979 television movie I Know Why the Caged Bird Sings, *Maya's mother (played by Diahann Carroll) tries to break through her daughter's silence. "To describe my mother would be to write about a hurricane in its perfect power. Or the climbing, falling colors of the rainbow," Maya Angelou wrote years later.*

attached a tablet and pencil to a belt for Marguerite to wear.

Despite Marguerite's silence, she and Bailey received a great deal of attention in the small, poor town. They were the two little travelers who had made it to a big city up North. People would stop by Momma's store, where the children worked after school, just to hear the tales Bailey wove about the elevators, flush toilets, Frigidaires, and skyscrapers of St. Louis. He had a lot to talk about, and since no one in Stamps knew any better, he could embellish his adventures as much as he wanted. Marguerite, however, remained silent. Most people assumed that she was pining for the big-city adventures she'd had.

Fortunately for Marguerite, one woman in Stamps saw her muteness for what it was. Bertha Flowers was Stamps's black aristocrat. "She was one of the few gentlewomen I have ever known," Maya recalled, "and has remained throughout my life the measure of what a human being can be. . . . It would be safe to say that she made me proud to be Negro, just by being herself."

Although Mrs. Flowers and Momma had frequent talks, they seemed so unalike that Marguerite wondered what they might have in common. One sunny afternoon when Mrs. Flowers stopped by the store, Momma told Marguerite to change into a good dress. She was to carry Mrs. Flowers's groceries home and stop in for a visit. Along the way, Mrs. Flowers spoke gently to Marguerite. She said that she knew Marguerite was doing well in school, but her teachers said it was difficult to get her to speak. She said that although no one could force her to speak, it was important to remember that language was mankind's way of communicating, a gift that separated humans from the lower animals. Mrs. Flowers also said that she knew Marguerite read a lot, but that reading out loud was what truly made words on a page come alive.

Intrigued, Marguerite listened silently.

Mrs. Flowers invited Marguerite inside her beautiful home for some lemonade and sweet vanilla cookies that she'd made especially for the young girl. She gave Marguerite some of her books and told her that she should read them aloud at home, trying to make each sentence sound different by changing her voice. She also gave the child a book of poems and asked her to pick one poem and memorize it just for her, so she could recite it the next time she visited.

Marguerite sat entranced as Mrs. Flowers read her the beginning of Charles Dickens's *A Tale of Two Cities*. "I heard poetry for the first time in my life," she later wrote in *I Know Why the Caged Bird Sings.*

Marguerite ran all the way home with the books she had been given and a batch of cookies made especially for Bailey. She was very happy. "I was liked, and what a difference it made. I was respected not as Mrs. Henderson's grandchild or Bailey's sister but for just being Marguerite Johnson," she remembers. With more visits and readings and pearls of wisdom from the wonderful special lady, Marguerite at last found her voice and a new self.

In a 1998 interview with the *New York Times,* Maya Angelou compared the trials of giving up muteness to those of overcoming drug addiction. For years after she began speaking again, Bailey and Vivian Baxter traveled to see her when misfortune struck, to make sure she would never sink into muteness again.

The next time Marguerite felt as special as she had with Mrs. Flowers, she was attending her grammar-school graduation from Lafayette County Training School in 1940. Her outstanding academic achievements and attendance record placed her among the first students to receive their diplomas. In fact, all of Stamps's young black population beamed in excitement and anticipation that day. "I had taken to smiling more often, and my jaws hurt from the unaccustomed activity," she recalled in *I Know Why the Caged Bird Sings*. "Lost tears were pounded to mud and then to dust. Years of withdrawal were brushed aside and left behind."

But graduation day was momentarily darkened by the address of the guest speaker, a white politician from out of town. The man told the students and their families about all the wondrous new improvements coming not to their school but to Central School—the white school in Stamps. The children going to that school would have new microscopes and chemistry equipment, among other luxuries. Of course, the speaker continued, he had to praise those children in front of him for having graduated a football player who had achieved fame at their Arkansas agricultural college. He also praised the gathered group for graduating some of the state's best basketball players.

In this man's mind, black children did not need to strive for academic greatness and scholarship. Their futures, he seemed to say, were limited to athletics; their dreams should not be the same as those of white children. The stunned audience fidgeted until the busy politician left the stage and hurried off to his next appointment.

But the crowd was heartened when the school's young valedictorian reclaimed the stage and led them all in an uplifting anthem. "While echoes of the song shivered in the air . . . the tears that slipped down many faces were not wiped away in shame," Maya recalled in her first auto-biography. "We were on top again. As always, again. We survived."

Survival, for Marguerite and her brother, continued when they were sent once more to live with their mother. Mrs. Henderson realized that as the children grew, they would have a better life away from the racial codes of the South that threatened to squelch their spirits—and that could also pose serious physical danger.

Maya Angelou says that her grandmother made the decision to return them to their mother after a horrifying experience of Bailey's. On his way home from the white section of Stamps, a white man forced the boy and a group of other blacks to retrieve the corpse of a drowned black man from the river and bring it to the local jail. It all seemed like a joke to the grinning man and to the white prisoners at the jail. Once home, Bailey could only ask Momma repeatedly why whites hated blacks so much. That very night, Maya believes, her grandmother began making plans to get the two children out of the South.

This time, Bailey and Marguerite found themselves in California, where their mother was now living. In Oakland, they went to a school that had a basketball court, a football field, and even ping-pong tables under awnings. No one checked up on how hard they were working, and Sundays were spent at the movies instead of at church. Despite the lack of supervision, Marguerite continued to do well in school, and she even began taking evening classes in drama and dance at the California Labor School, where she had earned a scholarship.

One summer, Marguerite traveled to San Diego to spend time with her father and his new girlfriend. But Marguerite could not get along with the young woman, who seemed only slightly older than she was. The young woman had presumed that Bailey's child was a young girl; she was surprised to meet someone of Marguerite's age. Bailey did nothing to ease the conflict, and after the two women ended up in a physical fight, Marguerite decided to set out on her own.

She spent a month sleeping in abandoned cars in a junkyard with some other homeless teens. The group developed a camaraderie that Marguerite had experienced only with her brother. Each of them was required to do

some odd job to pitch in for food. Impressed by the "community" she had joined, yet unwilling to believe that this was the best she could do, Marguerite finally called Mother for a plane ticket back to Oakland.

Marguerite moved into the 14-room boarding house where her mother had moved after marrying a successful businessman. The teenager's brief taste of freedom inspired her to abandon high school for a chance at

A few years after Marguerite and Bailey moved to Oakland to live with their mother, she spent a summer with her father in San Diego. The visit was a disaster; Maya ran away and lived in a junkyard with other runaways for a month before returning to her mother's home.

Maya Angelou sautés onions and peppers in the kitchen of a New York restaurant in 1997 as a "guest chef" for a dinner to benefit the Betty Shabazz Foundation. When she was 16 years old and a new mother, however, restaurant cooking was not something to smile about—it was hard work. The first job Maya took after her son, Clyde, was born was as a cook in a Creole restaurant; she had no experience but was told that Creole cooking simply involved using onions, green peppers, and garlic.

success outside the classroom, and she landed a job as a streetcar conductor for the Market Street Railway Company, the first black to do so, at only 15 years old (she had presented herself as 19).

After a semester, however, Marguerite returned to school. Riddled with confused feelings about growing up, she became pregnant from a single encounter with a popular boy. Her only interest in him was that he had agreed to help her find out what sex was like.

Marguerite managed to keep her pregnancy secret from her mother and her mother's husband until her high school graduation. Surprisingly, her mother was less upset than Marguerite had anticipated. Vivian Baxter had a way of seeing things pragmatically, according to Maya Angelou in *I Know Why the Caged Bird Sings*. She was always "hoping for the best, prepared for the worst, and unsurprised by anything in between."

Still young herself, Marguerite had much to learn about being a good mother. She saw her child as an extension of herself, a possession. "Just as gratefulness was confused in my mind with love, so possession became mixed up with motherhood," she wrote about the 1945 birth of her son, Clyde (later renamed Guy). "I had a baby. He was beautiful and mine. Totally mine."

Despite Vivian Baxter's adeptness at handling what life gave her, Marguerite felt that she and Clyde were infringing on Mother's charity, and two months after her son's birth Marguerite moved them out of the boarding house. Her mother found her a trustworthy baby-sitter, and Marguerite found a rented room and got a job as a Creole cook—even though she didn't know what Creole food was. She had simply seen a sign in a restaurant window advertising $75 a week for a Creole cook. Marguerite had managed to talk herself into many a job, and she told the person interviewing her that Creole was really the only style of food she knew how to cook. After she got the job, she promptly headed off to see a relative of Mother's whom she knew to be a good cook. He told her that making Creole food just meant cooking with onions, green peppers, and garlic. Marguerite figured she was prepared.

But after only a few months of being on her own, Maya found herself wallowing in the misery of being a jilted lover. When Bailey advised her to quit whining and do something about her situation, the young mother decided to move on. She headed to San Diego, where she found a new baby-sitter, a new job as a cocktail waitress, and a woman who agreed to tutor her in dance during the day. But her stay in San Diego didn't last long; after a few tumultuous months, she returned to her mother's home once again.

Mother welcomed her as though she had only been on a long vacation. Bailey was also living there while working as a waiter on the Southern Pacific Railroad. Marguerite easily found a job as a short-order cook in a dingy diner, but the job paid very little and left her depressed. She tried to escape her woes through music and books, and then, buoyed by Mother's encouragement that she "had great potential," she decided to join the Army's Officer Candidate School. There, she believed, she could not only learn a useful trade but also take advantage of the benefits offered to American soldiers by the GI Bill, which would allow her to return to school—and possibly buy a house—after she completed two years of service.

Just short of 19 years old, Marguerite was accepted by the school—and then rejected just one week before her induction. The school where she had taken drama and dance lessons a few years earlier was believed to be a Communist-front organization, and this affiliation was considered unacceptable for someone joining the Army.

Maya wrote in her second autobiography, *Gather Together in My Name,* that her life now had "no center, no purpose," and she took yet another job as a waitress. At the Chicken Shack restaurant, she began using marijuana in an attempt to ignore what appeared to be a very bleak future.

A publicity photo of Maya Angelou as an exotic dancer during the 1940s. For a time, her dancing jobs provided the only income for herself and her son.

3

ANYTHING FOR LOVE

"I was in a state again that was blood line familiar. Up a tree, out on a limb, in a pickle. . . . For the first time in my life I sat down defenseless to await life's next assault."

—*Gather Together in My Name*, 1974

MARGUERITE INNOCENTLY OPENED the door and spied a lean, long-faced man standing before her. He was looking for a dancer.

A dancer? She had maneuvered her way into an assortment of jobs, but she had never worked as a dancer. Of course, she had taken dance lessons since she was 14 and had become almost fanatical. Thinking about the pointlessness of her life right now—depressing hours working at the Chicken Shack—filled her with a desire to step beyond her limited world. There seemed to be no other choice than to tell this man that, yes, in fact, she was a dancer. She invited him in.

His name was R. L. Poole, and the people at the record shop that she frequented had given him her address. He was from Chicago, and he had contacts to get gigs but needed a female dance partner. He asked about her background, but Marguerite didn't have the right answers. She didn't do tap, jazz, or acrobatics. In a bold effort to save the moment, she proudly proclaimed that she knew other dances, that she "used to win every jitterbug contest," and that she could do a split. Determined to prove that final proclamation, she slid her legs into the beginnings of a split, fighting her straight skirt and unpracticed muscles while managing to keep her back straight, hold her arms in a graceful ballet pose, and even hum a tune.

But she still could not stretch all the way to the floor. As she struggled to complete the split, one leg became caught on the dining room table leg and the other on a gas pipe. She pulled her leg, but in the process yanked off the pipe, causing gas to hiss out and envelop the room. By then, R. L. had to intervene. He flung open the window, turned off the gas, and lifted the table so the teen could finally move her other leg.

Distraught, Marguerite feared that when she finally raised her head, R. L. Poole would be laughing at her. But he wasn't. "Well, anyway, you've got nice legs," he said simply, and he took her on as his new partner.

Once she was in an actual rehearsal hall, Marguerite was highly impressed by the seemingly reserved R. L. Indeed, he could move. In her role as his "flash" partner, she was to frame and highlight his tap dancing. She was dazzled. "To be able to let my body swing free over the floor and the crushing failures in my past was freedom," she wrote in *Gather Together in My Name.* "I thanked R. L. for my liberation and fell promptly in love with him."

Suddenly, life was a blast for Marguerite. Shortly after their first appearance together, R. L. and Marguerite landed their first club engagement, a two-week stint that excited Marguerite so much that she promptly quit her restaurant job to devote more time to practice. Marguerite knew that she could still count on Mother when she needed to borrow money during those months of practice before opening night. And while life with her beloved brother Bailey had been painful—he had grown remote and had developed a heroin habit—lately he had improved greatly. He was dating a delightful woman with whom he'd once gone to school. Bailey got clean, married Eunice, and rediscovered himself.

Unfortunately, R. L. and Marguerite's dancing prowess was going largely unappreciated. And then R. L.'s former girlfriend and dance partner, Cotton Candy Adams, arrived on the scene. When Marguerite met her, she realized she was out of a job. She also quickly saw that Candy was a serious drug user. Marguerite watched how Candy and R. L. moved and spoke to one another, and how eager they were to start dancing together. She couldn't understand why R. L. wanted to be with a drug user. And she couldn't figure out how this woman could muster up the energy to dance. But one thing was clear—Cotton Candy was in, and Marguerite was out.

After an exhausting period that Marguerite described as filled with weeping and self-pity, she decided to leave show business behind, at least for a time. She boxed up her tap shoes, which she would later write "hurt my feet anyway," and headed off to find a "real" job.

"Reality" took her and Clyde 80 miles east of San Francisco to Stockton, California. Her mother knew of someone there who needed a fry cook, and the opportunity provided a ready escape for Marguerite.

Marguerite's restaurant shift lasted from four until midnight, so she sent Clyde off to live with a baby-sitter. After her shifts, Marguerite would often get poufed and powdered and go out for a night on the town.

On one of these nights, she met L. D. (Louis David) Tolbrook, a smooth-talking, gambling man who was her father's age and had tailor-made clothes and manicured nails. Still in her late teens, Marguerite fell for L. D., who

Maya enjoyed the California nightlife in clubs like this one during her affair with L. D. Tolbrook, who promised he would leave his wife to be with her.

treated her well and gave her money to spend on Clyde and herself.

It didn't matter to Marguerite that L. D. was married. He told her that his wife was much older than he was, sickly, and a drug addict, and that he planned to leave her. For the next few weeks he took Marguerite along on "business rides" in his big silver-blue Lincoln. He never explained what kind of business he was in, and she wondered why he thought she was too "square" to understand. But it didn't matter. As time went by, she visited Clyde less frequently, and her restaurant job faded into the background. Even her favorite pastime—reading books— became unimportant to her. L. D. said that as soon as his divorce was finalized and he got his life in order, he and Marguerite could be "together forever."

But the romance was much more brief than that. After Marguerite hadn't heard from L. D. for a few days, he showed up at the restaurant and announced that he had accumulated a serious gambling debt—about $5,000. He had been trying to win enough money to send his wife back to Louisiana, he said. On top of that, he also owed the mob more than $2,000. Marguerite was shocked. What would they do?

L. D. described how the wife of a friend who was in similar trouble had once helped her husband by working briefly as a prostitute. In only one week, L. D. said, the woman had made $500. Of course, L. D. protested, he would never expect Marguerite to do something like that.

But of course she would do it, Marguerite said, and she told herself that she would maintain her integrity in the process. After all, she thought, she was doing it for a good purpose. She was happy that he would allow her to help him.

Yet helping L. D. was more difficult than Marguerite had expected. She had no desire to discuss her life with L. D. with the other women in the house of prostitution where she ended up living. And she had no desire to listen to the women talk about life with their pimps, whom they bragged about for providing them cocaine and beating them only when necessary, but never badly enough to leave scars. Disillusioned with her attempt to help L. D., Marguerite withdrew. She was not the temptress that men were looking for.

And then, Marguerite received word that her mother was lying ill in a San Francisco hospital after surgery and that she was asking for her daughter. Marguerite quickly made arrangements to return home by bus. Her regular baby-sitter, a woman named Big Mary, readily agreed to watch Clyde while Marguerite visited her mother. Since Marguerite had no phone number for L. D., she left a message with his landlord and left for San Francisco.

Marguerite arrived home to hear that Bailey's wife, Eunice, had died that very day of tuberculosis. It had just been the first anniversary of their marriage. Bailey was sleeping in a chair in their mother's hospital room. When his sedative wore off and he woke up, Marguerite rocked his sobbing body. "His big wet black eyes looked at me wanting to believe I could do something for his grief. I knew I had no magic, when he most needed me," Marguerite related in *Gather Together in My Name*. They left the hospital and went home. "Bailey cried for two hours, unintelligible human sounds growled and gurgled from his throat," she said. "He closed in upon himself. . . . I lost part of my brother forever."

When Bailey learned that Marguerite was a prostitute, he was livid. Who had gotten her into this? What drugs had the pimp gotten her hooked on? he raged. Knowing the temper of the "old" Bailey, Marguerite agreed to return to Stockton for Clyde and come back to San Francisco. Without saying so, she told herself that she would wait for Bailey to cool off and then go back to L. D. and explain what had happened.

But when Marguerite arrived at Big Mary's house in Stockton to pick up her son, she saw to her horror that the windows and door of the woman's house were shut up with planks. What had happened? Where was her baby? Terrified, Marguerite spoke to a neighbor, who told her that she didn't know where Big Mary had gone but that the baby-sitter had a brother in Bakersfield, California. The neighbor offered to let the shaken mother call the police from her house.

But the idea of calling the police made Marguerite even more anxious. What would the police do if they learned she was a prostitute? They might put her in jail and take away her son. The only answer was to seek out L. D. for help.

The pretty woman who answered the door at L. D.'s home seemed about 30 years old. Marguerite gave her name and asked to see L. D. In a moment, L. D. slipped out the front door and pushed his face within inches of Marguerite's. Who did she think she was, he spat, a silly little whore with the gall to come to his house and speak to his wife? So, it became clear to Marguerite, there was no sickly, older wife.

Marguerite had fallen for one of the oldest cons in the book. "I detested him for being a liar and a pimp, but more, I hated him for being such an idiot that he couldn't value my sterling attributes enough to keep me for himself alone," Marguerite wrote about L. D. in *Gather Together in My Name*. But Maya realized that, at the time, she herself was guilty of greed, "the greed which coerced me to agree with L. D.'s plans in the hope that I'd win . . . a life of ease and romance."

Refusing to succumb to despair, Marguerite focused on tracking down her child. She stayed that night in her rented room and headed for Bakersfield the following morning. With the help of local townspeople, she found the farm where Big Mary had moved, and as she approached in a cab she spotted her son standing in the mud in front of the farmhouse. "He kissed me and then started crying," she related in *Gather Together in My Name*. She continued:

> He took a fistful of my hair and twisted and pulled, crying all the time. . . . I stood holding him while he raged at being abandoned. My sobs broke free on the waves of my first guilt. I had loved him and never considered that he was an entire person. Separate from my boundaries, I had not known before that he had and would have a life beyond being my son, my pretty baby, my cute doll, my charge. . . . He was three and I was nineteen, and never again would I think of him as a beautiful appendage of myself.

Still determined to continue on her own, Marguerite returned briefly to San Francisco. Her beloved brother Bailey never fully recovered from the blow of losing his wife. He returned to using heroin, and though in her books

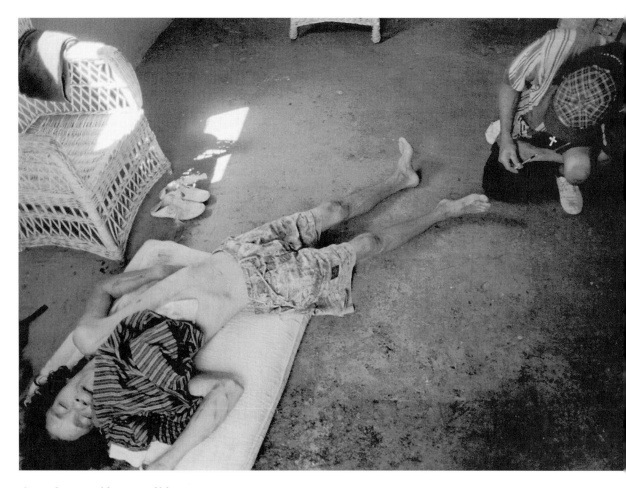

Gaunt heroin addicts in a filthy slum. A friend named Troubadour Martin, who was addicted to heroin, showed Maya the ugly effects of the drug and made her promise never to use it. "I had walked the precipice and seen it all," she later wrote of the experience, "and at the critical moment, one man's generosity pushed me safely away from the edge."

Maya says only that he committed crimes against property, not people, he served several jail sentences.

While in San Francisco Marguerite took and lost a few good jobs before getting one with a man named Troubadour Martin, who sold stolen women's clothing. He was kind and generous to her, but Marguerite, still in search of romantic love, was disappointed when he did not share her feelings.

Troubadour Martin was also a junkie. When she pressed Martin about wanting to share his life with her, he took her to a "shooting gallery," a term used to describe a gathering place for drug abusers who inject drugs.

Even Marguerite's active imagination could never have pictured the place where Troubadour took her. Inside a battered hotel room along the waterfront, Martin and Marguerite entered a room filled with seemingly comatose junkies, slumped over and leaning against the walls. Troubadour made her watch as he shot himself with heroin, suddenly unaware of the pain and ugliness he was showing her.

As Martin's face slackened, he asked her to promise that she would never use this drug. She promised. By exposing her to the brutal reality of his life as an addict, Martin had extended a kindness to her that she would never forget. "The life of the underworld was truly a rat race, and most of its inhabitants scurried like rodents in the sewers and gutters of the world," she wrote years later. "I had walked the precipice and seen it all; and at the critical moment, one man's generosity pushed me safely away from the edge."

Maya Angelou has detailed the struggles of her life in her five autobiographical works. In Singin' and Swingin' and Gettin' Merry Like Christmas *(1976) she recalled the ups and downs of her years working and raising her son in San Francisco.*

4

EUROPE FOR A SONG

"Music was my refuge. I could crawl into the spaces between the notes."

—*Singin' and Swingin' and Gettin'*
Merry Like Christmas, 1976

"HOW CAN YOU like someone you don't know?" Marguerite asked. "Because my heart tells me and I trust my heart," said the short, blonde, perfumey Louise Cox. Louise was co-owner of the Melrose Record Store in San Francisco, a popular attraction for musicians, music lovers, and collectors, where one was always sure to find copies of any recordings by black artists.

In Maya Angelou's third autobiography, *Singin' and Swingin' and Gettin' Merry Like Christmas*, she described her misgivings about meeting Louise, a white woman who Marguerite was surprised to find was actually friendly to her. To Marguerite, it didn't seem possible that Louise could like her without really know-ing her well. But Louise proved that it was possible.

First, Louise let Marguerite take some records on credit; shortly thereafter, she offered her a job as a sales-person. Marguerite was surprised and thrilled. Not only would she be able to listen to music all day—a favorite pastime—but she also could quit her two jobs at a real estate office and a downtown dress shop. She hoped the new job would help her forget the struggles she had had with L. D. and Troubadour Martin on the other side of the San Francisco Bay.

Still, Marguerite found it hard to trust Louise's friend-ship. She figured that it would just be a matter of time before Louise would show her prejudice toward blacks, so she listened and waited . . . and waited. But after two months on the job, she had not heard or seen anything that proved her point. Finally, she decided to relax and enjoy her musical oasis. Though she still had reservations about completely opening up to Louise, she was grateful for the job.

In a 1987 interview with the *Yorkshire Post*, Maya Angelou described the suspicion with which she viewed whites while growing up: "When I was a child I didn't think they were human. No members of the human race could behave as they did," she said. "Now I share the view of Terence, the Roman playwright who was himself a freed African slave, and who wrote, 'I am a human being therefore nothing human can be foreign to me.'"

Marguerite's job became a welcome retreat from the days when she was not working. On the evenings before her days off, she would pick up her screaming five-year-old son from the baby-sitter and wrestle his grip from her hem and legs as she paid her weekly bill. Crying hyster-ically as he was carried down the street, he would even-tually loosen his stranglehold on her neck and walk the rest of the way to her rented room. Once inside, the child followed her every move, fearful that any turn of hers might be a turn out the door without him.

The young mother spent her days off in the park, the zoo, or another inexpensive or free attraction that she thought would hold Clyde's interest. At night, Clyde would fight sleep in an effort to spend every possible moment with his mother. In the morning, he'd begin crying a few blocks before Marguerite reached the baby-sitter's house. "My own tears stayed in check until his screams stabbed from behind the closed doors and stuck like spearheads in my heart," Maya wrote of this torturous time in *Singin' and Swingin' and Gettin' Merry Like Christmas.* "The regularity of misery did nothing to lessen it."

Desperate to relieve Clyde's trauma, Marguerite considered her options. Welfare, she thought, was out of the question. She explained her attitude years later: "My pride had been starched by a family who assumed unlimited authority in its own affairs. . . . There was no motive on earth which would bring me, bowed, to beg for aid from an institution which scorned me and a government which ignored me."

Another option was to find a husband, who could provide security and a better way of life for her and Clyde. But finding a "husband-caliber man" seemed nearly impossible; in *Singin' and Swingin',* Maya speculated that it was perhaps her coolness or neediness that seemed to keep men at arm's length. In any event, she wrote, they were "rarer than common garden variety unicorns." Finally, hesitantly, she once again asked her mother whether she and Clyde could stay with her. This time, Marguerite promised to pay room and board.

While Vivian Baxter took her daughter and grandson in and life was more manageable for Marguerite, it wasn't

As a child, Marguerite Johnson had believed that white people were not human; in San Francisco, she discovered whites who treated her and Clyde with friendliness and respect. She fell in love with and married a white man, a former sailor named Tosh Angelos.

long before her situation began to wear on her. For two years, she wrote, she and her son "spun like water-spiders in a relentless eddy." Clyde was being tended to after school by the 75-year-old Poppa Ford, who lived at Mother's house. But the elderly man, his head bobbing with sleep each evening, was hardly a companion to her each night after she put her son to bed. Marguerite could not rely on Bailey for company, since he had taken off, and her mother was nearly always out at clubs or gambling in the evenings. During her shifts at the record store, the lonely single mother took to playing saccharine love songs to comfort herself.

One day, Marguerite was surprised to see a white man

enter the record store. The sight was unusual—the neighborhood was predominantly black, and most people thought of the jazz music sold in the store as being of interest to blacks only. Yet the man soon became a regular customer. He told Marguerite that he had been discharged from the Navy and was happy to have found a room in the neighborhood and a decent job in an electrical appliance shop. Still, Marguerite remained curious. Who was this white man who didn't mind living among blacks?

As they got to know one another, Marguerite realized that the man, a Greek whose name was Tosh Angelos, was wooing her through her son. Clyde, hungry for attention and comfort, was smitten. Tosh taught him how to throw a ball, took him to Fisherman's Wharf and to the zoo, and told him that he could be a ship's captain, a cable-car conductor, a lion tamer, or whatever else he wanted to be when he grew up.

Marguerite found Tosh appealing too—but she still felt great reservations. After all, she thought, what common ground could she have with a white man, part of the race whose members seemed to feel they had the right to abuse blacks for no reason? She wrestled with this question as her heart warmed toward Angelos. Still, she was unprepared when he asked her to marry him. Fiercely opposed to the idea, her mother ranted—and moved to Los Angeles just three days before the ceremony.

At first, Marguerite's new life with Tosh seemed to match her dreams of married bliss. The couple rented a large apartment, and Marguerite quit her job at the record store. At last she was a true housewife with a loving, reliable, and appreciative husband. Initially, Marguerite took comfort in Tosh's restrictions against visitors and making new friends. And though she was disturbed by his refusal to let her attend church and his insistence that they raise Clyde as an atheist, she interpreted this as Tosh's effort to envelop his family in a "cocoon of safety."

Eventually, however, the strain of trying to be happy began to show. Marguerite had always found comfort in believing herself a "child of God." She felt that this identity was part of her black heritage, and she wanted Clyde to experience it as well. She worried that being raised by a white man would diminish Clyde's sense of pride in his black ancestry. As a result, Marguerite began lying to Tosh. She went to church without him knowing.

Eventually, Tosh discovered what she was doing and confronted her. "I made no protest, gave no confession— just stood silent. And allowed a little more of my territory to be taken away," she explained in *Singin' and Swingin'*. "A bizarre sensation pervades a relationship of pretense. No truth seems true. . . . When our marriage ended completely, a year later, I was a saner, healthier person than the young, greedy girl who had wanted a man to belong to and a life based on a Hollywood film, circa 1940."

But comforting her son over his loss and reweaving the worn threads of their relationship was a great deal of work. Once more feeling abandoned, Clyde had to be reassured repeatedly of his mother's devotion to him. After all, if she could stop loving Tosh, to whom she was married for three years, couldn't she stop loving him, too? With much attention and warmth, Marguerite strengthened her bond with Clyde.

She also needed to find a new job in a hurry. She landed a job as a dancer—albeit in a somewhat questionable establishment called the Garden of Allah—but it got her back on stage and gave her a chance to vent some emotion and practice her footwork. Six times a week, she would perform six shows, each 15 minutes long. During breaks, she was required to hustle men at the bar into buying her drinks, for which she would earn a percentage of the sales.

To Marguerite, the salary and tips she received seemed like a fortune. Finally able to afford luxuries, she spent her money on fancy restaurants, new clothes for Clyde and

herself, and some new furniture. She even managed to save a few dollars for a future vacation. Marguerite eventually earned a reputation for being the best dancer in the place, and her straightforwardness with the bar customers earned her more tips than any of the other dancers.

Within three months of starting, however, Marguerite was fired. The other dancers had wrongly charged that her appeal was the result of her sleeping with the customers. Still, the

Marguerite took a job as an exotic dancer; within three months she was considered the best dancer in the establishment. However, the other dancers, jealous of the attention and money she was receiving, complained to the manager, forcing him to fire her.

owner agreed to keep Marguerite on a week-by-week basis if she had trouble finding another job. Luckily, she didn't.

Some of her fans at the Garden of Allah were entertainers and employees of the popular nightclub called the Purple Onion, in the city's North Beach section. When they heard she had lost her job, they invited her to take the place of their singer, who had gotten a better job in New York City. Marguerite knew she could sing—she had done so as a child in her grandmother's church—but she had no idea whether she was any good. She had never learned to sing with a piano accompaniment, and she had no professional experience.

But her energy and her dramatic expressiveness during the audition earned her a six-month contract with a three-month option to perform calypso songs at the Purple Onion. She was assigned a voice coach, and the pianist created her lead music. When told that she had to learn at least 12 songs before opening night, she did just that. And when the club's management told her to come up with a more glamorous name, she obeyed. Her stage name, "Maya Angelou," was created out of her brother Bailey's childhood nickname for her and a more exotic version of her married name.

"Popularity was an intoxicant and I swayed drunkenly for months," the newly named Maya Angelou revealed years later. "Newspaper reporters began to ask for interviews. . . . Fans began to recognize me in the street and one well-to-do woman organized a ten-member Maya Angelou fan club." As a performer, she was unflappable: when she would forget the words to her songs, she would simply dance more. Her coach and the club's owner were initially distressed, but when they observed the audiences' enthusiastic responses, they advised her: keep dancing more. Before long she was also composing her own songs by setting to music the lyrics of her own poems.

Maya's local stardom attracted the attention of several talent scouts. With a few months to go in her contract with

The manager of the Purple Onion cabaret gave Marguerite Johnson her first singing job. He also suggested that she change her name to something more exotic-sounding: Maya Angelou.

the Purple Onion, she met Robert Breen, the producer for a traveling opera company. He convinced her to audition for a part in the company's production of *Porgy and Bess,* George and Ira Gershwin's folk opera that tells the tale of the tragic love of Porgy, a handicapped black beggar, for the beautiful and unfaithful Bess. Members of the cast introduced her to a voice teacher, Wilkie, who planned to stay in the San Francisco area after the group went on tour and who agreed to tutor Maya. Eventually, Wilkie would meet Vivian Baxter, who had returned to San Francisco to open a restaurant. Mother had so much in common with Wilkie that she invited him to live in her home, and he became a dear family friend.

When Maya was offered a spot in *Porgy and Bess,* she explained her contractual agreement with the Purple Onion. The producer told her that the troupe would remain in San Francisco for two months to complete auditions before returning to Europe. At least she still had a chance.

Three days before her contract finally ran out at the Purple Onion, she had not heard from the casting director of *Porgy and Bess.* But she received a phone call from a New York theater producer, Saint Subber, who invited her to audition for a new Broadway show called *House of Flowers.* Marguerite felt torn. She was still hoping to hear from the *Porgy and Bess* director, and she didn't feel ready for the hustle of New York City. Nevertheless, Wilkie and her mother urged her to take the opportunity offered her rather than wait for one that might not materialize.

Within days of auditioning for *House of Flowers,* Maya received word that she had gotten a part. She had no sooner hung up the phone to share the news with her family when it rang again. She had been accepted for a role in Breen's *Porgy and Bess.* The company was now in Montreal, Canada, and would leave for Italy in four days. They were scheduled to perform in 15 cities in 10 different countries. In Maya's mind, there was no question which role she would take: she started to pack for Europe almost immediately after she hung up the phone.

Maya's one regret in this turn of events was that her touring with Breen's troupe meant leaving Clyde behind. When she telephoned her family to relate the most recent news, the boy asked whether she would be sending for him soon after her departure. Maya told him that though she couldn't send for him right away, she would be doing so soon. Welling inside Maya were her own feelings of having been abandoned by her mother at a young age. And here she was, she feared, inflicting the same pain on Clyde.

She promised herself that someday she would take her son to all the places she would be visiting with the troupe. But actually, it would be more than a year before Maya would see her son again.

Maya met up with the troupe in Montreal. She would make her debut once they reached Europe. Heartened by

An interracial dance club in Paris, France. The city was just one of the stops for Maya and the cast of Porgy and Bess *on their 15-city international tour in 1954–55.*

TWENTY-ONE CURTAIN CALLS

George Gershwin "never quite ceased to wonder at the miracle that he had been [the] composer [of *Porgy and Bess*]. He never stopped loving each and every bar, never wavered in the conviction that he had produced a work of art." So said Gershwin's first biographer, David Ewen. Indeed, George Gershwin was immediately intrigued by the novel *Porgy,* written by DuBose Heyward, when he first read it in 1926. He had quickly contacted the author to suggest that they collaborate on adapting a folk opera from its pages. Gershwin became immersed in the project, living on a South Carolina island while he researched his characters, and even joining—and winning—a drumming contest there with Gullah blacks (the name given to inhabitants of the region).

But Gershwin's enthusiasm was somewhat dampened when *Porgy and Bess* opened in New York in 1935 to critical disapproval. Many reviewers and audience members balked at what they believed were stereotyped views of blacks. Then, in 1937, before the show reached the height of its enduring success, Gershwin died of a brain tumor at the age of 38.

In time, though, the play's raw emotional vitality won the hearts of critics and audiences. By the time the Everyman's Opera Company began its overseas tour (which later included Maya Angelou), the musical had received 21 curtain calls in Berlin, Germany, according to an October 1952 report in *Musical America*. Meanwhile, tickets in Vienna, Austria, were being sold on the black market for the equivalent of a week's pay. "The ensemble was flawless," said *Musical America* about the Vienna performance. "Even minor characters like the street vendors crying their wares received bursts of applause."

the warm greetings of her colleagues, she quickly developed close friendships with three of the female singers. She reveled in watching the show from behind the stage, and she felt as inspired by it as she had been the first time she watched it in San Francisco.

Opening night in Europe was a smashing success. The troupe stayed in Venice for one sold-out week and was hailed by everyone from city officials to gondoliers. Singing in this country proved a great challenge for the American performers. "The Italians were the most difficult audiences to sing for," Maya related in *Singin' and Swingin'*. "They knew and loved music; operas, which

This photo of the first stage performance of the popular musical Porgy and Bess *was taken by the composer, George Gershwin.*

were mainly for the elite in other countries, were folk music and children's songs in Italy. They loved us, we loved them. We loved ourselves. It was a certainty: if Italy declared us acceptable we could have the rest of Europe for a song."

They were equally successful in Paris, France, where they extended their original three-week tour into several months. Here Maya moved into a cheaper hotel than that of the other troupe members. The performers were being paid partly in the currency of the country they performed in and partly in U.S. currency. Maya was beginning to feel the strain of tight finances, since she had been sending all

of her U.S. currency home to help pay for Clyde's keep—
and to diminish her guilt over feeling like an inadequate
mother. While in Paris, she took a singing job at the Mars
Club to earn more money.

The next stop was Zagreb, Yugoslavia. Traveling in a
Communist country whose citizens lived under tight
government restrictions and often in extreme poverty
was an eye-opener for the Americans. The *Porgy and
Bess* company was the first group of American singers to
be invited behind the Iron Curtain, and they were moni-
tored very carefully. They were permitted to walk only
within a four-block distance of their hotel, and they were
required to be driven to and from the theater.

The poor townspeople who gathered outside the hotel's
lobby windows gawked at the all-black cast, but they
weren't the only ones who were full of curiosity. Maya
couldn't resist exploring the town. Adept at picking up
languages, she had taken a few lessons in Serbo-Croatian
while in a city they had visited previously. Emboldened by
her new language skills, she made her way through the
crowd outside the hotel to a small music shop, where she
purchased a mandolin while under constant scrutiny from
the shopkeeper's wife and children. Finally, Maya tried
to speak with them. She was amazed to hear the woman
pronounce the name of Paul Robeson, a great African-
American singer, actor, and activist—and to hear the
woman begin singing a black spiritual:

> [The woman] began to sing "Deep River." Her husky voice
> was suddenly joined by the children's piping "My home is
> over Jordan." . . . They knew every word.
>
> I stood in the dusty store and considered my people,
> our history and Mr. Paul Robeson. Somehow, the music
> fashioned by men and women out of an anguish they
> could describe only in dirges was to be a passport for me
> and their other descendants into far and strange lands and
> long unsure futures.

"Oh don't you want to go/To that gospel feast?" [they sang]. . . . I made no attempt to wipe away the tears. . . .

My mind resounded with the words and my blood raced to the rhythms. . . . The storekeeper and his wife embraced me. My Serbo-Croatian was too weak to carry what I wanted to say. I hugged them.

By the time Maya had spent a year away from home, she had begun thinking about returning. Every letter she received from her nine-year-old son ended by asking whether he could come visit her or whether she would soon be home. When she received word that Wilkie had moved out and that her mother's restaurant was failing, forcing Vivian to find new work, Maya decided it was time to come home. Her mother was planning to take a job in a Las Vegas, Nevada, casino, and there would be no one to take care of Clyde.

But Maya had loved being away from home. Now in her mid-twenties, she had had the freedom to send money home for her son's care while staying out nights and going to clubs with her friends. Although the work was hard, in some ways it had seemed more like a party.

When she arrived in San Francisco, however, the guilt she felt over having left her son for so long intensified. In her absence, he had developed a serious and persistent rash and was now in constant fear that she would leave him again. But Maya reassured the boy that she would never again leave without him, and she finally saw him recover.

Though Maya moved to New York in the late 1950s to launch a writing career, she continued to perform in theater, and once received an invitation to sing at the legendary Apollo Theater in Harlem. Shortly after, Maya became involved in the civil rights movement.

5

BITING THE
BIG APPLE

"The world was on fire."

—*The Heart of a Woman*, 1981

"THEY HAD STRIPPED me, flayed me, utterly and completely undone me," Maya Angelou wrote about the reactions to a play she had written and read to members of New York City's Harlem Writers Guild.

After returning from her tour with the *Porgy and Bess* troupe, Maya and her son (who was now called "Guy" because the preteen said it was "less mushy" than Clyde) had hauled their luggage around the West Coast and Hawaii, following job leads for nightclub singers. Gradually, she achieved the economic independence she had strived to reach for so long. In 1958, after a brief stint on a houseboat commune, they had lived for a time on the outskirts of Hollywood and then in Westlake, California, a comfortable, friendly, and racially mixed neighborhood near Los Angeles. There, for the next year or two, in between out-of-town bookings at various nightclubs, Maya began to write.

Writing song lyrics had renewed Maya's interest in composing poetry and short stories. While in Hollywood, she met John Oliver Killens, a black novelist who was on the West Coast to write a screenplay. Impressed with her writing skills, Killens urged her to move to New York and join the Harlem Writers Guild, an informal group of writers who met regularly to read and offer constructive criticism of one another's work. Maya had already been considering a move to New York, and when her friend Abbey Lincoln, the jazz singer and actress, also encouraged her to do so, she needed no further incentive. She and Guy headed for the East Coast and settled in Brooklyn, New York.

Maya had attended three meetings of the Harlem Writers Guild before reading her own work, yet she was unprepared for the stinging criticism she received that night. In *The Heart of a Woman* she relayed the comments of her harshest critic: "'*One Life. One Love?*' His voice was a rasp of disbelief. 'I found no life and very little love in the play from the opening of the act to its unfortunate end.'"

But with encouragement from other members, Maya's anger and embarrassment waned. She knew that the people in the room were talented (the famed James Baldwin was part of the group) and that the advice was not really so very different from comments she had received from John Killens. She already had written and recorded six songs for Liberty Records and had written some short sketches and stories. Maya now realized that she had been careless in her writing, and she resolved to hone her skills. "Making a decision to write was a lot like deciding to jump into a frozen lake," she wrote in *The Heart of a Woman*. "If I survived at all, it would be a triumph. If I swam, it would be a miracle."

The Harlem Writers Guild did more than encourage black writers. Maya forged new friendships with interesting people like comedian Godfrey Cambridge and various other black artists, who introduced her to the burgeoning civil rights movement taking hold across the country. Finally, it seemed, good things began happening.

In addition to writing, Maya had also earned a couple of singing gigs at local clubs, including the famed Apollo Theater in Harlem. Performing in the same venue as jazz greats Pearl Bailey, Dizzy Gillespie, Count Basie, and Duke Ellington was an honor. During rehearsal, the theater manager warned her not to close with her usual finale, in which she solicited the audience's participation in a song called "Freedom." She would "die" up on stage if she tried, the manager told her. But Maya wasn't ready to listen. While the crowd for her opening performance was small, it was exceptionally responsive, and she felt sure that her finale would succeed. In *Heart of a Woman*, she described the audience's reaction:

> I explained, "If you believe you deserve freedom, if you really want it, if you believe it should be yours, you must sing." . . . The audience sang passionately. . . .
>
> By evening of the first day, I saw the power of the black grapevine. During the six o'clock show someone screamed from the audience, "Sing Freedom, Sing Freedom." . . . The audience pounded out the rhythm, moving it, controlling and possessing the music, the orchestra and me. . . . As the song ended the small crowd thundered a hot appreciation. . . . For six days and three shows per day, the tumultuous response was repeated.

But freedom was not just the title of a song. Across the country, blacks were joining the battle for civil rights that had long been denied them:

• On a bus in Montgomery, Alabama, in 1955, a woman named Rosa Parks decided to take a front seat, reserved only for whites. When Parks was arrested, a 27-year-old Baptist minister named Martin Luther King Jr. led blacks in a 382-day boycott of the city's bus system. A system of car pools was organized to take blacks to and from work, but many walked. Many of the protesters were jailed, and bombs tore apart King's house and four churches. Yet the bus system was eventually declared desegregated, and later the U.S. Supreme Court ruled segregation of public transportation unconstitutional.

• Inspired by the success of the Montgomery boycott, King called 60 southern black leaders to Atlanta and formed the Southern Christian Leadership Conference (SCLC), a network of local groups dedicated to non-violent demonstrations against civil rights violations. The SCLC continues its work today.

• In 1957, in Maya's home state of Arkansas, a vicious mob of cursing and spitting whites surrounded nine black students trying to enter Little Rock's Central High School. Governor Orval Faubus called in the National Guard and kept the students out, defying a 1954 U.S. Supreme Court ruling that desegregated public schools. President Dwight D. Eisenhower issued an immediate order to end any obstruction of integration, and the following day the president authorized 1,000 federal troops to accompany the students into the school building. Still, according to the October 1997 issue of *The Crisis,* a 1959 Gallup poll showed Governor Faubus just below Pope John XXIII and Billy Graham on a list of the 10 most admired men in the world. In 1965, more than 75% of the school districts in the Deep South were still segregated.

- In February 1960, four black students in Greensboro, North Carolina, refused to leave the white section at a segregated lunch counter, launching the beginning of numerous "sit-ins" throughout the South. By August that year, lunch counters in 15 cities had been desegregated. Through the beginning of 1961, more than 50,000 people took part in demonstrations of some sort in hundreds of cities.

When Maya and her friend Godfrey Cambridge first heard Martin Luther King Jr. speak in New York in 1960,

Physically shielded by the National Guard but exposed to taunts and verbal abuse, Elizabeth Eckford passes through a group of angry protesters as she enters Little Rock High School in 1957. The battle to desegregate schools in Arkansas, where Maya Angelou had grown up, was one of the first major confrontations of the civil rights movement.

As the civil rights movement gained momentum in the 1960s, thousands of African Americans throughout the United States participated in demonstrations designed to make others aware of racial inequality. In this November 1962 photo, blacks in Little Rock, Arkansas, demand service at a "whites only" lunch counter.

they too felt drawn to act. "He said the South we might remember is gone," Maya recalls of Dr. King's speech that day:

> There was a new South. A more violent and ugly South, a country where our white brothers and sisters were terrified of change, inevitable change. They would rather scratch up the land with bloody fingers and take their most precious document, the Declaration of Independence, and throw it in the deepest ocean, bury it under the highest mountain, or burn it in the most flagrant blaze, than admit justice. . . . We, the most hated, must take hate into our hands and by the miracle of love, turn loathing into love.

Maya and Godfrey were so moved by King's words that they decided to support the cause in the way they knew best—through theater. Together, they produced a revue that employed Godfrey's friend Hugh Hurd as director and many of Maya's acquaintances from her *Porgy and Bess* days. They paid union wages and donated the remainder of their profits to King's SCLC.

The show, *Cabaret for Freedom,* opened at the Village Gate, a famous club in Greenwich Village whose owner knew one of the leaders of New York's SCLC branch and was glad to offer the facility. The opening-night audience included Harlem politicians, successful black actors such as Sidney Poitier and Ossie Davis, and Lorraine Hansberry, author of the award-winning play *A Raisin in the Sun.* The cabaret ensemble earned an enthusiastic standing ovation.

The club's owner agreed to let *Cabaret for Freedom* use his place for five weeks and offered his extensive mailing list to them as well. For the remainder of its run, the show continued to fill the Village Gate to capacity. Many of the performers, somewhat impoverished but proud to be contributing to the civil rights movement, donated some or all of their pay to the SCLC.

By the time the show closed at summer's end in 1960, the performers weren't the only ones struggling financially; Maya was as well. Fortunately, the leaders of New York's SCLC invited her to take the job of office manager. In addition to administrative duties, she would also handle fund-raising chores, such as contacting philanthropists and arranging speaking engagements. Although she'd had a broad variety of jobs in her life, Maya was uncertain whether she could take on this responsibility—but as always, she agreed to try. Besides, she decided, the opportunity to work for Dr. King, one of her heroes, was well worth the modest pay she would earn.

After two months on the job, Maya returned from her lunch break one day to find her hero sitting at her own desk. King had wanted to meet her, he said, and he thanked her for her hard work. Maya struggled to speak. After all, it wasn't every day that a human legend walked right into your office. "He had an easy friendliness, which was unsettling," she wrote in *The Heart of a Woman*. "Looking at him in my office, alone, was like seeing a lion sitting down at my dining-room table eating a plate of mustard greens."

Dr. King made himself comfortable on the old sofa in her office and asked about her upbringing and her family, sounding not like a legend or a minister but an ordinary young man. When Maya spoke of her grandmother and uncle back in Stamps, "he nodded as if he knew them personally." When she found herself telling him that Bailey was in jail for selling stolen goods, "the personal sadness he showed . . . put my heart in his keeping forever." She had heard that Dr. King was an amazing man in many ways; now she knew for sure.

Not long after this meeting, Hazel Grey, one of Maya's SCLC workers, told her about a South African freedom fighter, Vusumzi Make, who reminded Hazel of Dr. King. Make was a representative of the radical Pan-African Congress, and he was in the country to address the United Nations about South Africa's horrid treatment of blacks. Hazel invited Maya to accompany her and her husband to hear Make lecture. But Maya was forced to turn down the offer. The famed "rat pack" of Hollywood—Frank Sinatra, Sammy Davis Jr., Joey Bishop, and Peter Lawford—were giving a benefit at Carnegie Hall for the SCLC, and there was still much to be done. There would be other opportunities to hear him speak, Maya told herself.

Maya little realized that the next opportunity would be a personal introduction to Make. Her friend John Killens and some of his colleagues had arranged a night at the Killens's home with both Vusumzi Make and Oliver Tambo, the leader of the less radical African National Congress. Within moments of being introduced, Maya

Dr. Martin Luther King Jr., third from left, in a photo from the 1963 March on Washington. Maya was inspired when she heard the great civil rights leader speak in 1960; she and a friend produced a benefit show to support his organization, the SCLC. After the successful five-week run of Cabaret for Freedom, *Maya was offered a job with the New York SCLC office.*

and "Vus" grew enchanted with one another. She found his accent delicious, his intelligence exciting, and his confidence intense. Make later asked Maya's friend whether Maya was married.

Actually, Maya was now engaged—to Thomas Allen, a bail bondsman whom she had met in a local bar. Allen saw her inspiring civil rights work with the SCLC as just a job;

he didn't talk much, and he and Maya had almost nothing in common. Yet Maya's ongoing dream of a quiet, secure marriage had by now grown from an intermittent tug to an insistent yank, and even though she had only known Thomas a very short time, she had agreed to marry him. Maya had already begun questioning her decision to marry Thomas when she met Vusumzi.

With her wedding day only two months away, Maya was nevertheless captivated by Vus. Her excitement grew when they met again at a party the next evening and at the annual black-tie ball sponsored by the American Society for African Culture a few days after that. Maya had arrived with her friend Rosa and Rosa's escort; Thomas was working late that night. Within moments, Maya was dancing with Vus. "I intend to change your life," he told her. "I am going to take you to Africa."

After that night, a circumspect Maya turned down Vus's invitations for lunch, but she was lavished with bouquets of flowers whose cards read, "From Vusumzi Make to Maya Angelou Make." When she finally succumbed and had lunch with him, Vus once again proclaimed his love and need for her. So intense was his pleading that Maya agreed to marry the freedom fighter she had met only a week before. Within days, Vus whisked her away with him to London for a conference. "I am marrying you this minute," he told her on the plane to England. "We never mentioned the word marriage again," Maya wrote in *The Heart of a Woman.*

When the conference ended, Maya returned to New York by herself and found an apartment, as Vus had directed. He had business to attend to for the Pan-African Congress and would be away, initially, in Cairo, Egypt. During the month that he was abroad, she settled into their new place with Guy. When Vus returned, the two thrilled to hear of his adventures and his decision that they would eventually move to Cairo.

Once again, however, Maya's dream of a blissful domestic life was shattered by reality. Only a day after returning home, Vus criticized Maya's decorating tastes and immediately rushed out to buy new furniture, paying for it with a huge wad of money whose source he refused to explain. Vus was fascinating and exciting, and he seemed to be an exceptional father, but he was so finicky that Maya began to wilt under the constant criticism. "Sometimes he would pull the sofa away from the wall to see if possibly I had missed a layer of dust," she wrote years later. "If he found his suspicions confirmed, his response could wither me. I was unemployed but I had never worked so hard in all my life."

Maya Angelou in 1970, the year I Know Why the Caged Bird Sings *was published and nominated for a National Book Award.*

6

ABUSED TOO LONG

"I can't deny it. When he starts talking about all that's been done to us, I get a twinge of hate."

—Dr. Martin Luther King Jr., speaking about
Black Muslim leader Malcolm X

"THE HONORABLE ELIJAH Muhammad offers the only possible out for the black man. Accept Allah as the creator, Muhammad as His Messenger, and the White American as the devil. If you don't believe he's a devil, look how he's made your life a hell."

So thundered Malcolm X, a powerful leader of the Nation of Islam (also called the Black Muslims), an organization that proclaimed all whites as devils and blacks as the rightful owners of the world. As Malcolm X spewed these stinging words on a Harlem street corner, the black crowd that had gathered around him shouted its support.

In *The Heart of a Woman,* Maya recalled that day in
1961 when she first heard the Black Muslim leader speak.
She and her friend Rosa stayed within hearing distance of
Malcolm X, but were kept from the platform on which he
stood. Several television crews and nervous white policemen surveyed the platform as well. The Nation of Islam's
promise that blacks would once again recover their rightful
place in the world was accompanied by the call to lead a
disciplined, committed life focused on family and duty.
Despite warnings from Nation of Islam founder Elijah
Muhammad, the group's national leader, Malcolm X, had
determined that he would bring attention to his organization with proud, inflammatory preaching.

Although Malcolm X would eventually be betrayed by
the organization he so boldly promoted and would under-
go a radical change in attitude toward whites, he was at the
time almost the exact philosophical and political opposite
of Martin Luther King Jr. While King advocated love as a
weapon to fight racial hatred, Malcolm X delivered fiery
predictions of doom for those that opposed the Nation of
Islam's teachings.

That day, Malcolm X's powerful words hit home even
more strongly. There had been a murder: Patrice Lumumba,
a freedom fighter in the African Congo and a hero of
blacks around the world, had been arrested and then died
mysteriously. Lumumba had become increasingly mili-
tant against the Belgian government of the Congolese
people. The area had been under white control for more
than 400 years, beginning with the stifling colonization
of the Portuguese in the 15th century and followed by
Belgian rule since 1907. When the Congolese finally won
their independence from Belgium in June 1960, Lumumba
was appointed the first prime minister of the Independent
Republic of the Congo.

Given only six months to institute its own government,
the Congo was unprepared when freedom arrived. A serious
uprising developed in Katanga, a large province intent upon

African freedom fighter Patrice Lumumba (right) is taken to prison by followers of Joseph Kasavubu. After the 1961 murder of Lumumba, who had been named the first prime minister of the Independent Republic of the Congo, Maya helped plan a nonviolent protest of his death at a United Nations General Assembly.

secession. Lumumba declared a state of emergency and called on the United Nations (UN) and the Soviet Union for assistance. Although he quelled the uprising, he was subsequently dismissed by Congolese president Joseph Kasavubu, and power was gained by Joseph Mobutu, an army leader who received strong U.S. support. Lumumba was construed to be anti-Western, yet his supporters argued that he was intent only on nonalignment and true independence.

Lumumba was arrested by Kasavubu's army and turned over to the Katanga regime. Some reports claimed that he was murdered by the separatists. Others said villagers killed him, and still others said he was killed while trying to escape the Katanga leaders. Lumumba's supporters believed that the Congolese government was responsible for the act; some believed that the United States and the United Nations shared some blame. While the facts were disputed, Lumumba's loss was a great tragedy for black activists around the world.

Maya and Rosa felt compelled to act. They took the news of Lumumba's death to a hastily called meeting of the Cultural Association for Women of African Heritage (CAWAH), a women's activist group they had established with their friend Abbey Lincoln only a few months before. The talented black women of the CAWAH promoted and raised funds for black civil rights organizations.

Of the 10 women who met that day at Maya's apartment, four disagreed that action was necessary and left. Those who remained decided to stage a silent protest at the United Nations session in which Lumumba's death would be announced.

Vus was away in India, but Maya remembered his advice about engaging in public protests: never do it on your own; let the masses hear about it and know who you are. When she shared his advice with Rosa, the two decided to visit Mr. Micheaux's bookstore in Harlem, a frequent black rallying spot, to ask him to spread the news about their protest. Instead, Micheaux told them to speak in his store that evening.

Maya and Rosa hardly expected the crowd that overflowed from the bookstore that night. Nor did they expect to see so many people gathered at the United Nations building on the morning of the demonstration. The protesters squeezed together on the sidewalks and were pressed into the street. Some carried placards; all of them were looking for direction, since UN guards would not allow them into the building. Rosa had been able to procure only seven tickets from delegates she knew, so she managed to usher people inside in groups of seven while Maya tried to calm the angry crowd outside.

By the time the session was scheduled to begin, about 75 protesters had made it inside. Maya was one of the last to get through the door. As U.S. representative Adlai Stevenson rose to speak, someone let out a piercing scream. "Murderers!" others cried, while the scream continued. Shocked, Stevenson stared toward the raucous crowd in the balcony as the lights came up in the room.

Maya was shaken. The last thing they wanted was to start a riot, but that's what was happening. A stampede for the doors began as one woman grappled with a guard in the aisle. Rosa and Maya urged everyone in their group to go outside, where they expected the atmosphere to be safer.

They were unprepared for the hostile mood of the crowd outside the UN building, which had grown in number in the short time they were inside. Having heard about the chaos inside, the crowd began moving toward the Belgian consulate a few blocks away, singing a black freedom song as they went. Heavily armed and tense, policemen and plainclothes officers followed.

Once there, Maya and another organizer managed to elude the security personnel in the building's lobby, but finally abandoned their effort to reach the authorities. Outside, television and radio reporters scoured the crowd for comments, and though CAWAH members had agreed not to speak to the press, others vented their rage. Shortly thereafter, the crowd dispersed, disappointed that they had come away with nothing but sore feet and taut anger.

After watching the news reports that night about the incident, Maya and other CAWAH members discussed the reaction of the crowd. In fear that these seething emotions would eventually cause people to turn against one another, they agreed to arrange a meeting with Malcolm X, in the hope that he could offer guidance.

U. S. ambassador Adlai Stevenson discusses the situation in the Congo in a February 1961 United Nations Security Council meeting. The protest planned for the UN debate drew many more people than Maya and fellow organizers had expected, and it nearly turned into a riot.

"After I knew Malcolm would see us I became appalled at our presumption," Maya related in *The Heart of a Woman*. As the meeting time drew closer, she became nearly speechless, but Rosa maintained her composure. "He approached, and all my brain would do for me was record his coming," Maya wrote. "I had never been so affected by a human presence. . . . His hair was the color of burning embers and his eyes pierced."

But his advice was not what the women expected. "You were wrong," he said. Demonstrating at the United Nations would never win freedom for anyone, he told them. Nor would it prevent the deaths of more black leaders, be they

African or American. Himself a skilled manipulator of the media, Malcolm X predicted that other black leaders would condemn the demonstration—not for the reasons he had just outlined, but because they wanted to look good in the white man's eyes by denying that blacks were truly angry. These leaders would distance themselves from the CAWAH by labeling it dangerous, Malcolm X declared.

But the Black Muslim leader offered more than disheartening pronouncements. He was determined to offer blacks the freedom that came from the teachings of the Nation of Islam. More important, he offered to make a statement to the press regarding the UN incident. "I will say that yesterday's demonstration is symbolic of the anger in this country," he told them. "That black people were saying they will not always say 'yessir' and 'please, sir.' And they will not always allow whites to spit on them at lunch counters in order to eat hot dogs and drink Coca-Colas." Though they were encouraged by Malcolm X's words, Maya and the other CAWAH members also saw his predictions about the other black leaders come true.

Maya once again found herself on stage in May 1961, when she took her husband's advice and became involved in Jean Genet's play *The Blacks*, which opened off-Broadway at St. Mark's Playhouse. Among the members of the strong cast were Cicely Tyson, Lou Gossett Jr., and James Earl Jones. *The Blacks* carried a strong message. It warned of what could happen when the oppressed were no longer persecuted, of their eventual control over former authorities, and their adoption of the appalling behavior and beliefs of their own oppressors.

Maya also continued writing and attending meetings of the Harlem Writers Guild. At home, however, her life was once again in turmoil. She watched as her teenage son grew closer to Vus and more distant from her. And she found that Vus had not been faithful to her. When she confronted him with evidence, he adamantly denied the accusations.

In 1961, Maya appeared in Jean Genet's The Blacks, *a play that warned of the dangers of oppression. The cast included several other talented African Americans who would achieve stardom, including Cicely Tyson, Lou Gossett Jr., and James Earl Jones.*

Maya was crushed and did not know what to do. She wrote in *Heart of a Woman:*

> Separation was not possible. Too many friends had advised me against the marriage, and my pride would not allow me to prove them right. Guy would never forgive me if I moved us one more time and I couldn't risk losing the only person who really loved me. . . . There was a sad irony in the truth that I was happier in the dusty theater than in my pretty apartment on Central Park West. . . . I started going to the theater early and returning home reluctantly

But even Maya's place of refuge was soon closed to her. She had been financially mistreated by the producer of *The Blacks*, and Vus sent an angry telegram telling him she wouldn't be back. Although Maya felt vindicated by Vus's action, she was also left without a job, forced to rely on parceled-out money from her husband. Already feeling distanced from her family, she withdrew from her friends and even from the Harlem Writers Guild.

One night Maya came home to a final eviction notice tacked on the apartment door. Vus must have received the previous warnings and kept them hidden, she thought; she had always felt unsteady about not being allowed in on their financial situation, and this notice proved that her misgivings had been well-placed. When Vus came home and told her not to worry, she found it difficult to take his advice.

Vus put his wife and her son in a hotel and then headed off to Egypt to arrange for their move to Cairo. Still battling a tangle of mixed emotions, Maya boarded a plane with Guy to meet her husband. Her first sight of Vus in the hubbub of Africa brought a rush of reassurance. "I had no doubt, for the moment, that we were going to make each other frivolously happy," she wrote later. "Cairo was going to be the setting for two contemporary lovers." Even Guy was excited to settle in their new home, and he became his old self again and did well in his new school.

But it wasn't long before Maya realized that they were in grave financial difficulty again. Despite the extravagant evenings of entertainment and the lavishly decorated apartment, they were two months overdue on their rent, and behind on payments for the exquisite rugs and antique French furniture.

Maya sought help from David Du Bois, an American whom she had befriended in Cairo. Du Bois got her a job as an associate editor covering African affairs on the *Arab Observer*, a relatively new magazine that presented the Egyptian government's perspective.

When Maya explained to Vus that she had gotten a job to help them out of their financial predicament, he exploded. She was not to work outside the home, he railed. Who was she to think she shouldn't consult him on such a decision? As Maya listened to his diatribe, she realized that she had handled the situation poorly. She also realized that she was no longer in love.

Pressed by others to try and get their relationship to work, Vus and Maya stuck it out for another six months, but to no avail. Maya told Vus that she was moving to Ghana with her son; Vus got plane tickets and arranged for them to stay with friends once they arrived. Maya and Guy were on a new adventure once again. When she saw the relief on her son's face, she realized that the boy had been struggling too.

Ghana in 1962 was an exciting place to be. President Kwame Nkrumah, an African hero, was loved by blacks around the world. Ghana had only recently been established as a country in its own right; the areas that made up the new nation had gained their freedom from the British only in March 1957. In Ghana, blacks weren't relegated to jobs as maids, cooks, or other servants; they could be whatever they wanted to be. In her 1986 book, *All God's Children Need Traveling Shoes*, Maya related, "For the first time in our lives the color of our skin was accepted as correct and normal."

She knew she had made the right choice in moving to Ghana.

But shortly after their arrival, Guy was involved in a serious car accident. He drifted in and out of consciousness for a time as he was put into a body cast, and then an arm and leg cast. He was hospitalized for a month, and then was sent home for three months of recovery.

But they really hadn't found a permanent home yet. Though they were warmly accepted by friends and acquaintances in Ghana, Maya had moved into the YWCA and was quickly running out of funds. Fortunately, she got a job as an administrative assistant at the University of Ghana, where administrators arranged for Maya to live in the house of an instructor who was out of the country for six months.

Now of college age and completely healed from the accident, Guy enrolled at the University of Ghana. For the first time in years, he would live apart from his mother, in a campus dormitory. "He pulled me to him and wrapped his arms around me," Maya wrote, and said, "'I love you, Mom. Maybe now you'll have a chance to grow up.'"

At the university, Maya got involved in a performance of Bertolt Brecht's *Mother Courage*. She eventually moved into a pretty white bungalow with two other friends, both from the United States. Before long, the house was a meeting place for political discussion.

In 1964 Malcolm X came to visit the group at the home of activist Julian Mayfield, and people of varying political stripes gathered eagerly. What Malcolm X said was completely unexpected. He had made a pilgrimage to Mecca and was transformed, he said. "I met White men with blue eyes, who I can call brother with conviction. That means that I am forced to reconsider statements I have made in the past and I must have the courage to speak up," he said. He explained to the group that he now had a new plan, and he had already met with various African leaders to gain their support. He planned to go before the United Nations to condemn the United States for its racism. His listeners

Former Nation of Islam leader Malcom X (second from left) meets with traditional Muslim leaders in Cairo, Egypt, in 1964. Disenchanted with the separatist philosophy of the Nation of Islam, Malcolm had founded his own organization, Muslim Mosque Incorporated, and his journey to Mecca brought him closer to the views of nonviolent civil rights advocates such as Martin Luther King Jr. Eight months after this meeting, Malcolm X was gunned down during a speaking engagement in New York City by Black Muslim followers.

shouted agreement, and they offered to help him meet as many political leaders as possible.

Within a week they introduced him to Ghanaian cabinet members, the African and European Diplomatic Corps, and several ambassadors and other political figures. But no matter how much influence they exerted, they were unable to arrange for Malcolm to meet Ghana's president, Kwame Nkrumah. Finally Shirley Du Bois, the recent widow of W. E. B. Du Bois, took him to see Nkrumah. Maya was furious that the woman had waited so long to arrange the meeting. She mentioned her anger to Malcolm X, as she and Julian Mayfield were accompanying him to the airport to return to the United States. In *All God's Children Need Traveling Shoes*, Maya related Malcolm's response:

"Now, Sister, I thought you were smart, but I see you are very childish, dangerously immature." He had not spoken so harshly before to anyone in Ghana—I was shocked. . . . Tears were bathing my face. . . . "Don't be in such a hurry to condemn a person because he doesn't do what you do, or think as you think or as fast. There was a time when you didn't know what you know today." His voice had become more explanatory and less accusatory.

"I wanted to ride with you to encourage you to broaden your thinking. You are too good a woman to think small. You know we, I mean in the United States and elsewhere, are in need of hard thinkers. Serious thinkers, who are not timid."

Indeed, Malcolm had mentioned to them more than once that the United States needed their help. His letters from America relayed all sorts of news and asked for their support when he sent envoys to Africa. Eventually, Malcolm X asked Maya to return to the United States and work for his newly formed Organization of Afro-American Unity.

After long deliberation and discussion with Guy and her friends, Maya decided to take the offer. The ambivalence she felt upon watching her son grow to manhood would be easier to handle at a greater distance. All of those she consulted agreed that leaving Ghana then was the right thing for her to do. "If the heart of Africa still remained elusive, my search for it had brought me closer to understanding myself and other human beings," Maya later wrote. "The ache for home lives in all of us, the safe place where we can go as we are and not be questioned."

Maya Angelou told talk-show host Oprah Winfrey that the greatest moment in her life was when she realized, "I can do anything, anything I want to do."

7

THE GREATEST MOMENT

"Sometimes, people think that the public recognition is the greatest thing."

—Maya Angelou during a 1993 televised
interview with Oprah Winfrey

MAYA RETURNED TO the United States on Friday, February 19, 1965, excited at the prospect of working with the great black leader Malcolm X. She spoke with him the following day. But by Sunday, February 21st, the dream was dead. That day, Malcolm X was shot to death during a speaking engagement at Harlem's Audubon Ballroom, in front of his wife and four young daughters.

The tragedy convinced Maya to renounce a career in politics. She returned to the warmth of California, where she wrote a play, and in 1966 she took a part in a Hollywood production of *Medea.* That same year her play, a two-act drama titled *The Least of These,* was produced in Los Angeles, and Maya became a lecturer at the University of California at Los Angeles. Two years later, Maya wrote a 10-part television series comparing American life with African life.

Maya's continued friendship with author James Baldwin resulted in an introduction to Jules and Judy Feiffer. The Feiffers convinced a friend who worked for Random House to entice Maya to write an autobiography of her unusual and colorful life. For a woman who thrilled at the challenge of creating a sentence that was just right, the invitation to write a life story as though it were literature was too tempting to turn down.

Within a week of its publication in 1970, *I Know Why the Caged Bird Sings,* a memoir that focused on Maya Angelou's life up to her teens, became a national bestseller. In the first eight months of publication it was reprinted five times. Nominated for a National Book Award, the work remains her most acclaimed volume. That year, she also became a writer-in-residence at the University of Kansas and received a fellowship from Yale University.

From that breathtaking beginning, Maya went on to produce a bevy of additional bestsellers. She once said that because there are only two things that she truly loves to do—dancing and writing—she knew she would have to write when her knees gave out.

Only a year after her first book was released, Maya was nominated for the renowned Pulitzer Prize for her volume of poetry, *Just Give Me a Cool Drink of Water 'fore I Diiie.* By 1972 she had become the first black woman to have an original screenplay, *Georgia, Georgia,* produced.

In 1973, Maya married Paul Du Feu, a carpenter and construction worker whom she met in London. That same year she was nominated for a Tony Award for her Broadway

This photograph of Maya and her bestselling autobiography was taken in 1971, after she was hired to write and direct a TV film version of I Know Why the Caged Bird Sings. *She became Hollywood's first black woman director, also working on the TV movie* All Day Long *(1974). Twenty-four years later, she directed her first major film,* Down in the Delta *(1998).*

theater debut in *Look Away*. With a seemingly insatiable drive for ever more challenging projects, in 1974 she directed the film *All Day Long*. She was also named distinguished visiting professor at Wake Forest University, Wichita State University, and California State University at Sacramento. Maya Angelou's second autobiography, *Gather Together in My Name,* was also published in 1974, and the following year another book of poetry, *Oh Pray My Wings Are Gonna Fit Me Well,* was published.

In an interview 13 years later, Maya described her writing habits and schedule. She explained that she rises at 5:00 each morning and heads for a hotel room, where she can truly concentrate. She works from 6:30 until 12:30, lying across the bed and leaning on one elbow as she writes on yellow legal pads. She forces herself to leave the room by 12:30, having found that most of the writing done after that hour ends up being edited out anyway.

Upon returning home, she showers, puts on fresh clothes, and goes food shopping or plays solitaire. During peak writing times, she wears out two or three decks of cards a month. After dinner, she reviews the day's work. "If April is the cruelest month," she said in the 1987 interview, "then eight o'clock at night is the cruelest hour," speaking of the editing process she takes on each evening. For her efforts, she is usually left with three or four pages, out of the 10 to 12 that she completes each day. She has described the process of writing as similar to jumping into an ice-covered pool: "It sounds terrible," she says, "but once in it and two or three laps done, I'm home and free."

Ever undaunted by jumping into that ice-covered pool, Maya published her third memoir, *Singin' and Swingin' and Gettin' Merry Like Christmas,* in 1976. She appeared in the 1977 TV miniseries *Roots,* an adaptation of author Alex Haley's own memoirs, winning an Emmy Award nomination for her performance, and in 1978 published a collection of poetry, *And Still I Rise.* When *I Know Why the Caged Bird Sings* was made into a television movie in 1979, Maya wrote the script and music.

In 1981, the revered author became the first person to receive a lifetime appointment as Reynolds Professor of American Studies at Wake Forest University. Ever since, she has continued to teach and to lecture around the country. But happiness in love once again proved elusive: she divorced Paul Du Feu after eight years of marriage. A few years later, she would tell an interviewer that she didn't plan on marrying again; she didn't believe any man could help but feel threatened by her success. She described the pain of breaking up with someone as "absolutely obliterating. It tears me up. . . . I and romance have been thrown on the floor. I hang over the chairs. I weep."

In 1981 Maya faced another personal loss, the death of her mother, Vivian. She threw herself into her work, and between 1981 and 1993 she published nine more books, including her fourth and fifth memoirs, *The Heart of a Woman* (1981) and *All God's Children Need Traveling Shoes* (1986), and two volumes of poetry, *Shaker, Why Don't You Sing?* (1983) and *I Shall Not Be Moved* (1990). In 1983 she also wrote the screenplay for an NBC television program, *Sister, Sister.* In 1993, Maya shared the wisdom of her experience in a book for children called *Life Doesn't Frighten Me.*

Already the recipient of numerous awards, in 1993 Maya Angelou received another high honor—she was invited by president-elect Bill Clinton, a fellow Arkansan, to compose and recite a poem at his inauguration on January 20, 1993.

In a televised interview later that year with Oprah Winfrey, a woman whom Maya calls her "daughter-friend," Maya described the process of preparing for such an historical appearance. She explained that, being a child of God, she knew that she was up to the task, but first she had to wait for the life of the poem to "get into the marrow of my bones and into my fingernails—into my hair follicles." Once it was a part of her, Maya set to work writing it down. She retreated to her hotel room, where she filled reams of notepaper with observations about her country and its diverse beauty.

That cold morning of the inauguration, Maya faced a vast crowd gathered in the shadow of the Capitol and recited "On the Pulse of Morning." The poet had been chosen by Clinton because he believed that she embodied the brightest hopes for his administration. In 655 words, Angelou paid tribute to the multitudes of people from all races and cultures who have come to America to seek a better life. "Each of you is the descendant of some passed-on traveller," she told the audience. She also unsparingly criticized the country that could give rise to much misery in the name of greed and profit. Maya urged her fellow citizens to remember their shared history, "despite its wrenching pain," for "if faced/With courage, [it] need not be lived again."

Maya Angelou's pace did not slow after her appearance at the Capitol. In a 1998 interview with the *New York Times,* she admitted to being a "workaholic" and said she requires only four or five hours of sleep each night. Between 1994 and 1997, she published five books, including two more children's volumes, *My Painted House* and *My Friendly Chicken and Me.* She was one of the few women invited to address the Million Man March in Washington, D.C., in 1995, where she read her poem "From a Black Woman to a Black Man" before the thousands of black men gathered there. That same year, she read another of her poems, "A Brave and Startling Truth," at the 50th anniversary celebration of the founding of the United Nations. In 1998, at age 70, she directed her first major film, *Down in the Delta,* starring Wesley Snipes and Alfre Woodard, which was released at the same time as her son Guy's first novel.

Maya's works continue to sell quite well. In 1997, Oprah Winfrey chose *The Heart of a Woman* as one of her Oprah Book Club selections, sending the title to the top of

bestseller lists and increasing the number of copies in print to more than one million. Maya's 1997 collection of essays, *Even the Stars Look Lonesome*, reached bestseller lists even before her national publicity campaign began, causing Random House to increase its print run from 350,000 copies to 375,000.

In reviewing her life and accomplishments during the 1993 TV interview with Winfrey, Maya described her greatest moment. It wasn't the completion of the inaugural poem, nor the reading of it, although she explained that reading it had been a great, proud moment for which she

After being elected president in 1992, Bill Clinton emulated one of his personal heroes, former president John F. Kennedy, by asking an important American poet to compose lines to be read at his inauguration. Kennedy had asked Robert Frost in 1961; Clinton turned to fellow Arkansan Maya Angelou, who wrote "On the Pulse of Morning." Angelou read the short poem at the January 20, 1993, swearing-in ceremony.

Maya Angelou shows off her 1994 Grammy Award for Best Spoken Word or Non-Musical Album. Now in her seventies, Angelou has shown no sign of slowing down: she wrote five books between 1994 and 1997.

was most grateful. Instead, her greatest moment was an instance of private revelation, which occurred in 1953 when a teacher had her read the phrase "God loves me" out loud. He made her read it again and again and again. Finally, he stopped her. "Try to know it," he told her.

During the interview, Maya's eyes filled with tears at the memory of this experience. "Oprah, Oprah," she said in her rich voice, wanting to take her friend back to that day. Each time she recalls that moment, she said, "the skies open up." It was then when she felt that she truly understood the meaning of that simple statement: "I can do anything, anything I want to do, anything good, anything helpful. I can do it."

"You see," she said, "that is the greatest moment."

CHRONOLOGY

1928	Born Marguerite Johnson on April 4 in St. Louis, Missouri, to Bailey and Vivian Baxter Johnson
1931	With brother, Bailey, sent to live with paternal grandmother in Stamps, Arkansas
1936	With Bailey, returns to St. Louis to live with her mother; is raped by her mother's boyfriend. Both children are returned to Stamps; severely traumatized, Marguerite does not speak for about five years
1940	Graduates from Lafayette County Training School; moves to San Francisco to live with her mother
1944	Works as a conductor on San Francisco cable cars
1945	Graduates from Mission High School; her son, Guy, is born
1949	Marries Tosh Angelos; divorces two-and-a-half years later
1953	Performs at the Purple Onion nightclub in San Francisco; adopts stage name of Maya Angelou
1954–55	Tours internationally with the Everyman's Opera Company production of *Porgy and Bess*
1959	Moves to Brooklyn, New York, and joins the Harlem Writers Guild
1960	Coproduces, directs, and performs in *Cabaret for Freedom;* selected as a regional coordinator for the Southern Christian Leadership Conference; appears in *The Blacks*
1961–62	Moves to Cairo, Egypt, with South African freedom fighter Vusumzi Make; becomes associate editor for the *Arab Observer*
1963–65	Serves as administrative assistant at the School of Music and Drama, University of Ghana; is feature editor for the *African Review* and contributor to the *Ghanaian Times* and Ghanaian Broadcasting Company
1970	First autobiography, *I Know Why the Caged Bird Sings,* is published and nominated for National Book Award; becomes writer-in-residence at University of Kansas; is granted Yale University fellowship
1971–72	First volume of poetry, *Just Give Me a Cool Drink of Water 'fore I Diiie,* is published and receives Pulitzer Prize nomination in 1972; becomes first black woman to have original screenplay produced with *Georgia, Georgia*
1973	Nominated for a Tony for her Broadway debut in *Look Away;* marries Paul Du Feu

1974 Second autobiography, *Gather Together in My Name,* is published; becomes distinguished visiting professor at Wake Forest University, Wichita State University, and California State University

1975 *O Pray My Wings Are Gonna Fit Me Well,* a collection of her poems, is published

1976 Third autobiography, *Singin' and Swingin' and Gettin' Merry Like Christmas,* is published

1977 Receives Tony Award nomination for her role in TV miniseries *Roots*

1978 *And Still I Rise,* a book of her poems, is published

1981 Fourth autobiography, *The Heart of a Woman,* is published; divorces Paul Du Feu

1982 Appointed chair in American Studies at Wake Forest University; writes *Sister, Sister* for NBC

1983 Publishes *Shaker, Why Don't You Sing?,* a collection of poems

1986 Fifth autobiography, *All God's Children Need Traveling Shoes; Mrs. Flowers: A Moment of Friendship;* and *Poems: Maya Angelou* are published

1987 *Now Sheba Sings the Song* is published

1990 Collection of her poems, *I Shall Not Be Moved,* is published

1993 Reads her poem "On the Pulse of Morning" at the inauguration of Bill Clinton; *Wouldn't Take Nothin' for My Journey Now; Soul Looks Back in Wonder;* and children's book, *Life Doesn't Frighten Me* are published; plays small role in and contributes poetry for film *Poetic Justice*

1994 *The Complete Collected Poems of Maya Angelou* is published; publishes two children's books, *My Painted House* and *My Friendly Chicken and Me*

1995 *Phenomenal Woman: Four Poems Celebrating Women* is published; reads "A Brave and Startling Truth" at the celebration of the 50th Anniversary of the United Nations; reads "From a Black Woman to a Black Man" at the Million Man March in Washington, D.C.

1996 Children's book, *Kofi and His Magic,* is published

1997 Collection of essays, *Even the Stars Look Lonesome,* is published

1998 Directs first feature film, *Down in the Delta*

FURTHER READING

Bates, Daisy. "The Long Shadow of Little Rock." *The Crisis*, October 1997.

Besharov, D. J. *Recognizing Child Abuse: A Guide for the Concerned*. New York: Free Press, 1990.

Elliot, Jeffrey M., ed. *Conversations with Maya Angelou*. Jackson: University Press of Mississippi, 1989.

Franklin, V. P. *Martin Luther King Jr.* New York: Park Lane Press, 1998.

Gioseffi, Daniela, ed. *On Prejudice: A Global Perspective*. New York: Doubleday, 1993.

Hansberry, Lorraine. *A Raisin in the Sun*. New York: New American Library, 1959.

McPherson, Dolly. *Order Out of Chaos: The Autobiographical Works of Maya Angelou*. New York: Peter Lang, 1990.

Meltzer, Milton, ed. *The Black Americans: A History in Their Own Words, 1619–1983*. New York: Harper Trophy, 1987.

Morgan Willis, Corinne, ed. *Dear Diary, I'm Pregnant: Teenagers Talk About Their Pregnancy*. Buffalo, New York: Firefly Books, 1997.

Patrick, Diane. *Amazing African American History: A Book of Answers for Kids*. New York: John Wiley & Sons, 1998.

Weisbrot, Robert. *Marching Toward Freedom: From the Founding of the Southern Christian Leadership Conference to the Assassination of Malcolm X (1957–1965)*. Philadelphia: Chelsea House Publishers, 1994.

Zinn, Howard. *A People's History of the United States*. New York: HarperCollins, 1990.

APPENDIX

CHILD SEXUAL ABUSE: THE FACTS

Note that figures based on reported cases are usually much lower than those obtained from surveys, and more than one source claims that the surveys provide a truer picture of the extent of the sexual abuse problem in the United States. Part of the discrepancy between figures based on reported cases and those based on surveys arises from the fact that many cases go unreported. In addition, varying definitions of sexual abuse are used; for example, the definition cited by the U.S. government in its National Incidence Study (NIS) was more narrow than in most other sexual abuse studies.

- In 1997, approximately 84,320 new cases of child sexual abuse were accepted for service by child protective services agencies. [1]

- A 1995 Gallup Organization telephone survey indicated that 19 children out of every 1,000 had been sexually abused. [2]

- According to the U.S. government's NIS, which was based on actual reported cases of abuse, 217,000 children, or more than 3 out of every 1,000, were sexually abused in 1993. This number is up from 1.9 out of every 1,000 in 1986 and .7 out of every 1,000 children in 1980. [3]

- The increased number of children living in poverty and a decrease in economic resources for the poor also may have contributed to the rise in the 1993 NIS statistics. According to the study, children from the lowest-income families were 18 times more likely to be sexually abused. However, since compilers received more reports from lower-income groups on the average, the figure may also be skewed. [3]

- According to the 1993 NIS, girls were sexually abused three times more often than boys. [3]

- A 1985 survey by the *Los Angeles Times* found that at least 22 percent of Americans have been victims of child sexual abuse, although one-third of that number told no one until they were well into adulthood. Only 3 percent of these cases had ever been reported to the police.

- In 1979, in the first truly random study of child sexual abuse, Harvard Ph.D. Diana Russell found that 38 percent of those questioned had been sexually abused. She also found that, except during the two world wars, the percentage of girls "at risk" for incest grew from about 9 percent in 1916 to 28 percent in 1956.

Sources: 1. National Committee to Prevent Child Abuse, July 1998.
2. "Child Sexual Abuse" Fact Sheet. American Humane Association, Children's Division, November 1997.
3. Sedlak, Andrea J., and Diane D. Broadhurst. *The Third National Incidence Study of Child Abuse and Neglect.* U.S. Department of Health and Human Services, September 1996.

JUST FOR KIDS:
WHAT YOU CAN DO ABOUT CHILD ABUSE

■ WHAT IS CHILD ABUSE?

When parents or other adult caretakers deliberately harm a young person, it is child abuse. This harm can happen physically through hitting, beating, punching, and slapping, or it can happen sexually when an adult or older person has sexual contact with a young person. Harm can also come to a young person when the need for food, clothes, a place to live, or medical care or supervision are ignored by parents or an adult caretaker. This is called neglect.

Another form of child abuse is called emotional abuse. A parent or adult caretaker is emotionally abusing his or her child when the adult rarely has anything good to say to the child, refuses to speak to the child for days, or frequently threatens to hurt the child.

■ HOW CAN I PROTECT MYSELF FROM CHILD ABUSE?

- Pay attention to your feelings. Know what makes you feel happy, sad, scared, angry, or upset.

- Know yourself and do things that make you feel good about yourself. When you feel self-confident, it is harder for someone else to take advantage of you.

- Get to know a person before you agree to go anywhere alone with that person. Be sure someone else knows where you are going and when you should be back.

- Be aware and alert about people and places. If you feel unsure, get away and ask for help from someone you trust.

- Make a list of people you can talk to if you have a problem. Then if you or a friend has a problem, be sure to *ask for help* from one of those people!

■ WHAT CAN YOUNG PEOPLE DO ABOUT CHILD ABUSE?

Child abuse is a tough thing for a young person to talk about. It makes that person feel confused, embarrassed, and frightened. There are laws to protect young people against child abuse, but until the abuse is reported, no one may know that the young person needs help. The most important thing to do is to *tell someone about the abuse.* Here are some ways you can do so:

- Report child abuse directly to the police or to the local Child Protection Services office in your neighborhood (you can find the phone number in the yellow pages under "Child Abuse").

- Talk to an adult who works with young people, such as a favorite teacher, a youth worker, or a religious leader.

- Remember that child abuse *is never the child's fault.*

- Read about child abuse and neglect so you will be better prepared to help yourself and others. You can find information in your local library or on the Internet.

- Encourage your friends to get help if they need it. Be aware that child abuse and neglect can happen to anyone.

Source: Child Abuse Prevention Council of Montgomery County (Indiana), Inc.
(http://www.child-abuse.org/needknow.htm)

WHERE TO GET HELP FOR VICTIMS
OF CHILD ABUSE AND NEGLECT

**American Humane Association,
Children's Division**
63 Inverness Drive East
Englewood, CO 80112-5117
303-792-9900
http://www.amerhumane.org

Child Abuse Prevention Network
http://child.cornell.edu/

Childhelp USA
15757 North 78th Street
Scottsdale, AZ 85260
800-4-A-CHILD (422-4453)
http://www.childhelpusa.com

Child Welfare League of America
440 First Street, N.W., 3rd Floor
Washington, DC 20001-2085
202-638-2952
http://www.cwla.org

**National Center for Missing
and Exploited Children**
2101 Wilson Blvd., Suite 550
Arlington, VA 22201
800-843-5678

**National Clearinghouse on
Child Abuse and Neglect**
P.O. Box 1182
Washington, DC 20013-1182
800-FYI-3366 (394-3366)
http://www.calib.com/nccanch

**National Committee to Prevent
Child Abuse**
200 South Michigan Avenue, 17th Floor
Chicago, IL 60604-2404
312-663-3520
http://www.childabuse.org

**National Directory of Hotlines
and Crisis Intervention Centers**
Covenant House Nineline
346 W. 17th Street
New York, NY 10011
800-999-9999
TDD 800-999-9915

INDEX

PICTURE CREDITS

Pamela Loos has written numerous magazine articles. She is a graduate of Rutgers University, where she received a B.A. in English. Having taught high school, she has since pursued a career in publishing. Still in her bookcase is her first copy of *I Know Why the Caged Bird Sings,* from her high school days.

James Scott Brady serves on the board of trustees of the Center to Prevent Handgun Violence and is the vice chairman of the Brain Injury Foundation. Mr. Brady served as assistant to the president and White House press secretary under President Ronald Reagan. He was severely injured in an assassination attempt on the president, but remained the White House press secretary until the end of the administration. Since leaving the White House, Mr. Brady has lobbied for stronger gun laws. In November 1993, President Bill Clinton signed the Brady Bill, a national law requiring a waiting period on handgun purchases and a background check on buyers.